CREATIVE
DESTRUCTION

*How Globalization Is Changing the World's Cultures*

# CREATIVE
## DESTRUCTION
# TYLER COWEN

PRINCETON UNIVERSITY PRESS

PRINCETON AND OXFORD

Copyright © 2002 by Princeton University Press
Published by Princeton University Press, 41 William Street,
Princeton, New Jersey 08540
In the United Kingdom: Princeton University Press, 3 Market Place,
Woodstock, Oxfordshire OX20 1SY

Library of Congress Cataloging-in-Publication Data

Cowen, Tyler.
Creative destruction : how globalization is changing the world's
cultures / Tyler Cowen.
p. cm.
Includes bibliographical references and index.
ISBN 0-691-09016-5 (alk. paper)
1. Culture. 2. Globalization. 3. Cultural relations. 4. International relations
and culture. I. Title

HM621 .C69 2002
306—dc21          2001059166

British Library Cataloging-in-Publication Data is available
This book has been composed in Palatino by Gary R. Beck
Printed on acid-free paper. ∞

www.pupress.princeton.edu

Printed in the United States of America

10 9 8 7 6 5 4 3 2

A country that makes
a film like *Star Wars*
deserves to rule the world

— Philip Adams, then chairman of
the Australian Film Commission

# Contents

# ■ Acknowledgments

The author wishes to thank Bryan Caplan, Peter Dougherty, Eli Lehrer, Robin Hanson, Daniel Klein, Timur Kuran, David McBride, David Schmidtz, Daniel Sutter, John Tomasi, the commentators on my previous two books (whose comments have been directly relevant here), several anonymous referees, and various seminar participants and colleagues at George Mason University for comments and discussion. The Mercatus Center has supplied essential research support and funding for this project.

CREATIVE
DESTRUCTION

# 1
### ■ Trade between Cultures

Haitian music has a strong presence in French Guiana, Dominica, Martinique, Guadeloupe, and St. Lucia—the smaller Caribbean markets. Many Antillean musicians have resented the Haitian success, even though they derived many musical ideas from the Haitian style of compas (pronounced "comb-pa"). The founder of Kassav, the leading Antillean group in the funky style of zouk, stated: "It's this Haitian imperialism [i.e., the popularity of the groups] that we were rising against when we began Kassav." Governments responded with protective measures to limit the number of Haitian bands in the country. Ironically, Antillean zouk now has penetrated Haiti. Haitian musicians resent the foreign style, although like their Antillean counterparts they do not hesitate to draw on its musical innovations. Haiti's compas style was originally a modified version of Cuban dance music and Dominican merengue.[1]

The Canadian government discouraged the American book-superstore Borders from entering the Canadian market, out of fear that it would not carry enough Canadian literature. Canadians subsidize their domestic cinema and mandate domestic musical content for a

---

[1] On these episodes, see Guilbault (1993, chap. 5).

percentage of radio time, which leads to extra airplay for successful Canadian pop stars like Celine Dion and Barenaked Ladies. Americans take pride in the global success of their entertainment industry, but Canadian writer Margaret Atwood coined the phrase "the Great Star-Spangled Them" to express her opposition to NAFTA.

The French spend approximately $3 billion a year on cultural matters, and employ twelve thousand cultural bureaucrats, trying to nourish and preserve their vision of a uniquely French culture.[2] They have led a world movement to insist that culture is exempt from free trade agreements. Along these lines, Spain, South Korea, and Brazil place binding domestic content requirements on their cinemas; France and Spain do the same for television. Until recently India did not allow the import of Coca-Cola.

Trade is an emotionally charged issue for several reasons, but most of all because it shapes our sense of cultural self. More than ever before, we are aware that not everyone likes how international trade and globalization are altering today's cultures. The terrorist attacks of September 11, 2001, on America were directed first at the World Trade Center, a noted icon of global commerce.

Harvard philosopher Robert Nozick, in his *Anarchy, State, and Utopia*, argued that market society offered a cultural utopia based on freedom of choice. He portrayed a hypothetical libertarian world where individuals would freely choose their lifestyles, their mores, and their culture, so long as they did not impinge on the rights of others to make the same choices. Such a vision has held great appeal for many, but it has skirted the empirical question of how much choice actually is available in the market, or would be available in a more libertarian society.

Numerous commentators, from across the traditional political spectrum, have argued that markets destroy culture and diversity. Benjamin Barber claimed that the modern world is caught between Jihad, a "bloody politics of identity," and McWorld, "a bloodless economics of profit," represented by the spread of McDonald's and

[2] For data on French expenditures, see Drozdiak (1993).

American popular culture. John Gray, an English conservative, has argued that global free trade is ruining the world's polities, economies, and cultures. His book is entitled *False Dawn: The Delusions of Global Capitalism*. Jeremy Tunstall defined the "cultural imperialism thesis" as the view that "authentic, traditional and local culture in many parts of the world is being battered out of existence by the indiscriminate dumping of large quantities of slick commercial and media products, mainly from the United States." Fredric Jameson writes: "The standardization of world culture, with local popular or traditional forms driven out or dumbed down to make way for American television, American music, food, clothes and films, has been seen by many as the very heart of globalization."[3]

Alexis de Tocqueville, the nineteenth-century French author of *Democracy in America*, provided foundations for many modern critics of commercialism. Tocqueville is not typically considered an economic thinker, but in fact his book is permeated with a deep and original economics of culture; he provides the most serious nineteenth-century attempt to revise Adam Smith. He sought, for instance, to disprove the Scottish Enlightenment dictum that an increase in the size of the market leads to more diversity. For Tocqueville, market growth serves as a magnet, pulling creators towards mass production and away from serving niches. For this reason, Tocqueville portrayed America as producing a culture of the least common denominator, in contrast to the sophistication of European aristocracy. While Tocqueville's account of America was subtle and nuanced, and in many regards favorable, he believed that broader markets for cultural goods lowered their quality.

[3] See Barber (1995, p. 8), Tunstall (1977, p. 57) and Jameson (2000, p. 51). For related contemporary perspectives, see Tomlinson (1991), Robertson (1992), and Schiller (1992). Barnet and Cavanagh (1996) provide another clear statement of the typical charges leveled against cultural globalization. For a critique of Gray, see Klein (2000). The more general doctrine of primitivism found early expression in Rousseau's Noble Savage, and, going back farther in time, in the Greek view that historical change represents corruption and decay. Christian doctrine, especially the Garden of Eden and Man's Fall, provided inspiration for the doctrine that pure, original cultures are doomed to fall from grace. On the Christian roots of primitivism, see Boas (1948); on the history of the Noble Savage idea, see Fairchild (1961). On primitivism in classical antiquity, see Lovejoy and Boas (1965).

3

Given the recurring nature of such criticisms, we cannot help but wonder whether the market does in fact expand our positive liberties and increase the menu of choice. If not, the freedom to engage in marketplace exchange will stand in conflict with other notions of freedom, such as an individual's ability to choose or maintain a particular cultural identity. More generally, the question at stake is what kinds of freedom are possible in the modern world.

To pursue this issue, I ask some fundamental questions about culture in a market economy. Does trade in cultural products support the artistic diversity of the world, or destroy it? Will the future bring artistic quality and innovation, or a homogeneous culture of the least common denominator? What will happen to cultural creativity as freedom of economic choice extends across the globe?

Modern debates refer frequently to the buzzword of globalization. Commentators invest this term with many meanings, including the growth of world trade and investment, world government, international terrorism, imperialist conquest, IMF technocracy, the global arms trade, and the worldwide spread of infectious diseases. I make no attempt to evaluate globalization in all its manifestations, but rather I focus on the trade in cultural products across geographic space.

A typical American yuppie drinks French wine, listens to Beethoven on a Japanese audio system, uses the Internet to buy Persian textiles from a dealer in London, watches Hollywood movies funded by foreign capital and filmed by a European director, and vacations in Bali; an upper-middle-class Japanese may do much the same. A teenager in Bangkok may see Hollywood movies starring Arnold Schwarzenegger (an Austrian), study Japanese, and listen to new pop music from Hong Kong and China, in addition to the Latino singer Ricky Martin. Iraq's Saddam Hussein selected Frank Sinatra's "My Way" as the theme song for his fifty-fourth birthday.[4]

I focus on one particular aspect of culture, namely those creative products that stimulate and entertain us. More specifically, I treat

---

[4] Micklethwait and Wooldridge (2000, p. 190).

music, literature, cinema, cuisine, and the visual arts as the relevant manifestations of culture. Given this field of inquiry, I focus on how trade shapes artistic creativity in the marketplace.

I leave aside broader social practices. I do not consider how globalization influences family norms, religion, or manners, except as they may affect creative industries. These social practices, while relevant for an overall assessment of globalization, are outside my chosen purview. I focus on markets, rather than on peoples or communities per se. I consider what kinds of freedom are available *in the marketplace*, rather than what kinds of freedom we have *to remain outside the marketplace*. I do not, for instance, examine whether we should attach intrinsic value to preventing the commodification of global creativity.

Instead I treat international commerce as a stage for examining an age-old question, dating back at least as far as Greek civilization: are market exchange and aesthetic quality allies or enemies? Furthermore our look at markets, and the resulting menu of choice, will help address other questions from classic antiquity. Was Herodotus pointing to a more general phenomenon when he ascribed the cultural vitality of the Greeks to their genius for synthesis? Was Plutarch correct in suggesting that *the exile*, and the corresponding sense of foreignness, is fundamentally creative in nature, rather than sterile? Along the lines of the Stoics, to what extent should our loyalties lie with the cosmopolitan, or to what extent should they lie with the local and the particular?

## ■ Our Conflicting Intuitions

We have strongly conflicting intuitions about the worldwide trade in cultural products. On the plus side, individuals are liberated from the *tyranny of place* more than ever before. Growing up in an out-of-the-way locale limits an individual's access to the world's treasures and opportunities less than ever before. This change represents one of the most significant increases in freedom in human history.

5

More specifically, the very foundations of the West (and other civilizations throughout history) are multicultural products, resulting from the international exchange of goods, services, and ideas. To varying degrees, Western cultures draw their philosophical heritage from the Greeks, their religions from the Middle East, their scientific base from the Chinese and Islamic worlds, and their core populations and languages from Europe.

If we consider the book, paper comes from the Chinese, the Western alphabet comes from the Phoenicians, the page numbers come from the Arabs and ultimately the Indians, and printing has a heritage through Gutenberg, a German, as well as through the Chinese and Koreans. The core manuscripts of antiquity were preserved by Islamic civilization and, to a lesser extent, by Irish monks.

The period between 1800 and the First World War saw an unprecedented increase in internationalization. The West adopted the steamship, the railroad, and the motor car, all of which replaced travel by coach or slow ship. International trade, investment, and migration grew rapidly. The nineteenth century, by virtually all accounts, was a fantastically creative and fertile epoch. The exchange of cultural ideas across Europe and the Americas promoted diversity and quality, rather than turning everything into homogenized pap.[5]

Conversely, the most prominent period of cultural decline in Western history coincides with a radical shrinking of trade frontiers. The so-called Dark Ages, which date roughly from the collapse of the Roman Empire in A.D. 422 to early medieval times in 1100, saw a massive contraction of interregional trade and investment. The Roman Empire had brought regular contact between the distant corners of Europe and the Mediterranean; the Roman network of roads was without historical parallel. After the fall of the empire, however, trade dried up, cities declined, and feudalism arose as nobles retreated to heavily armed country estates. During this same period, architecture, writing, reading, and the visual arts all declined drastically. The magnificent buildings of antiquity fell into disrepair, or

---

[5] As a percentage of the world economy, international trade grew from 3 to 33 percent; world trade, as a share of world output, did not return to its 1913 levels until the 1970s. See Waters (1995, p. 67) and Krugman (1996, p. 208).

were pillaged for their contents. Bronze statues were melted down for their metal, and many notable writings perished.

The rise of medieval society and the Renaissance was, in large part, a process of reglobalization, as the West increased its contacts with the Chinese and Islamic worlds. At the same time, trade fairs expanded, shipping lanes became more active, scientific ideas spread, and overland trade paths, many dormant since the time of the Romans, were reestablished.

These successes did not involve cultural exchange on equal terms. To put it bluntly, the notion of a cultural "level playing field" is a myth and will never be seen in practice. Never did the Greek city-states compete on an even basis. Christian and Graeco-Roman cultures were entrenched in Europe partly by fiat. British culture has had a significant head start in North America. The benefits of cultural exchange usually have come from dynamic settings in great imbalance, rather than from calm or smoothly working environments.

"Third World" and "indigenous" arts have blossomed on the uneven playing field of today's global economy. Most Third World cultures are fundamentally hybrids—synthetic products of multiple global influences, including from the West. None of the common terms used to describe these cultures, whether it be "Third World," "indigenous," "original," or "underdeveloped," are in fact appropriate designations, given the synthetic nature of the creative arts.

To give one example, the sculpture of the Canadian Inuit was not practiced on a large scale until after World War II. Even the earlier, nineteenth-century carvings drew on sailors' scrimshaw art for inspiration. White artist James Houston, however, introduced soapstone carving to the Inuit in 1948. Since then the Inuit have created many first-rate works in the medium. The sale of stone-carved works in Western art markets, often for lucrative sums, also has allowed the Inuit to maintain many of their traditional ways of life. The Inuit have moved into printmaking as well, and with commercial and aesthetic success.[6]

---

[6] On scrimshaw art, see Furst and Furst (1982, p. 138); on the minor role of stone carving among the Inuit prior to Houston, see J.C.H. King (1986, pp. 88–89). Good general treatments are Swinton (1972) and Hessel (1998).

Analogous stories are found around the world. The metal knife proved a boon to many Third World sculpting and carving traditions, including the totem poles of the Pacific Northwest and of Papua New Guinea. Acrylic and oil paints spread only with Western contact. South African Ndebele art uses beads as an essential material for the adornment of aprons, clothing, and textiles. These beads are not indigenous to Africa, but rather were imported from Czechoslovakia in the early nineteenth century. Mirrors, coral, cotton cloth, and paper—all central materials for "traditional" African arts—came from contact with Europeans. The twentieth-century flowering of Third World "folk arts," prominent throughout the world, has been driven largely by Western demands, materials, and technologies of production. Charlene Cerny and Suzanne Seriff have written of the "global scrap heap," referring to the use of discarded Western material technology in folk arts around the world.[7]

World musics are healthier and more diverse than ever before. Rather than being swamped by output from the multinational conglomerates, musicians around the world have adapted international influences towards their own ends. Most domestic musics have no trouble commanding loyal audiences at home. In India, domestically produced music comprises 96 percent of the market; in Egypt, 81 percent; and in Brazil, 73 percent. Even in a small country such as Ghana, domestically produced music is 71 percent of the market.[8]

Most world music styles are of more recent origin than is commonly believed, even in supposedly "traditional" genres. The twentieth century brought waves of musical innovation to most cultures, especially the large, open ones. The musical centers of the Third World—Cairo, Lagos, Rio de Janeiro, pre-Castro Havana—have been heterogeneous and cosmopolitan cities that welcomed new ideas and new technologies from abroad.

[7] See Brunside (1997, p. 93), and Bascom (1976, p. 303). On the Ndebele, see Glassie (1989, p. 64). The artistic benefits of Western metal knives were widely recognized, including in such locales as Papua New Guinea, Melanesia, and New Zealand; see Weatherford (1994, pp. 250–51).

[8] See Cowen and Crampton (2001), drawing on UNESCO data from World Culture Report 2000, table 5.

In all of these examples, the notable creators are active, searching artists, drawing on many sources to produce the sought-after aesthetic effect. These points do not denigrate non-Western artists or imply that they "owe it all to the West." It is the contrary emphasis on monoculture that insults, by portraying non-Western artists as unchanging and static craftworkers, unable to transcend their initial styles for synthetic improvements.

Cinema is one of the most problematic areas for globalized culture, as we will see in chapter 4, due largely to the export success of Hollywood. Nonetheless in the last twenty years Hong Kong, India, China, Denmark, Iran, and Taiwan, among other locales, have produced many high-quality and award-winning movies. African cinema remains an undiscovered gem for most viewers, and European cinema shows signs of commercial revitalization. Hollywood cinema itself has relied on international inspiration from the beginning, and should be considered as much a cosmopolitan product as an American one.

American books do not typically dominate fiction best-seller lists abroad. At any point in time American books typically account for no more than two or three of the top ten best-sellers, if even that many, in countries such as Germany, France, Italy, Israel, the Netherlands, and the United Kingdom. The Netherlands is a very small country, with fewer than ten million people, but most of its best-sellers are of Dutch origin. Many people still prefer to read books written originally in their native language, and about their native culture. Even in Canada, American books do not typically command half of the fiction best-seller lists.[9]

Nor are the most influential books, in the international arena, necessarily from today's richest countries. Arguably the most influential books in the world remain the Bible and the Koran, neither of which is a Western product in the narrow sense, though the former has been shaped by Western interpretations.

[9] The magazine *The Economist* surveys international best-sellers on a periodic basis. Cowen and Crampton (2001) present one summary version of this information.

Western literature, as well as the bookstore and the modern printing press, typically has spurred native writers. Salman Rushdie of India, Gabriel García Márquez of Colombia, Naguib Mahfouz of Egypt, and Pramoedya Toer of Indonesia, among others, are world-class writers, comparable to the best of Europe and the United States, if not better. These fictional traditions, now worldwide, drew directly on Western literary models and institutions.

Appropriately, Third World writers have been some of the strongest proponents of a cosmopolitan multiculturalism. Salman Rushdie describes his work as celebrating hybridity, impurity, and mongrelization. Ghanaian writer Kwame Anthony Appiah believes that cosmopolitanism complements "rootedness," rather than destroying it, and that new innovative forms are maintaining the diversity of world culture. Rabindranath Tagore, Gandhi's foil earlier in the century, favored international trade and cooperation over national isolation or boycotts of foreign goods. He saw the genius of Indian society in synthesizing the cultures of the East and the West. Even the critics of globalization have, for the most part, been diverse products of a worldwide intellectual culture, strongly rooted in Western and classic Greek methods of analysis and argumentation.[10]

## ■ The Downside

Despite the triumphs of synthetic culture, we should not ignore the costs of cross-cultural exchange. Montesquieu wrote: "The history of commerce is that of communication among peoples. Its greatest events are formed by their various destructions and certain ebbs and flows of population and of devastations."[11]

[10] On Rushdie, see Waldron (1996, pp. 105–9). Also see Appiah (1992, 1998). On Tagore, see Sinha (1962) and Dutta and Robinson (1995). On the history of cosmopolitan thought more generally, see Wagar (1963). Montesquieu (1965 [1748], p. 24) saw the genius of the Romans in their synthetic abilities: "The main reason for the Romans becoming masters of the world was that, having fought successively against all peoples, they always gave up their own practices as soon as they found better ones."

[11] Montesquieu (1989 [1748], p. 357).

Globalized culture illustrates Joseph Schumpeter's metaphor of capitalist production as a gale of "creative destruction." Cultural growth, like economic development, rarely is a steady advance on all fronts at once. While some sectors expand with extreme rapidity, others shrink and wither away.

It is hard to argue that Polynesian culture is more vital today than several hundred years ago, even though the Polynesians are wealthier in material terms. Materialism, alcohol, Western technologies, and Christianity (according to some) have damaged the Polynesian sense of cultural potency. In Tahiti many creative traditional arts have been neglected or abandoned as they lost status to Western goods or proved uneconomical. Polynesian culture has hardly disappeared, but it now limps along on the margins of Western achievement.

Some commentators have suggested that China opened Tibet to the outside world, not out of tolerance and magnanimity, but to destroy the native culture. Coca-Cola and Western tourists may succeed in doing what decades of coercive Communist intervention failed to achieve—weakening traditional Tibetan attachments to their rich brocade of history, rituals, temples, and Buddhist religion. The Himalayan kingdom of Bhutan charges tourists two hundred dollars a day in the hope of maintaining a protected sense of identity. The country has no traffic lights and no city with more than ten thousand inhabitants. Wild dogs roam the streets. Poverty and malnutrition are rife, but the country maintains intense forms of Buddhist mythology and art that are perishing elsewhere.[12]

Travel puts the downside of cross-cultural exchange right before our eyes. Even travelers of only moderate experience complain that their fellow countrymen have "spoiled" various locales or diminished their authenticity. Sophisticated travelers go to great lengths to seek out places that are otherwise undertouristed, precisely for their unique qualities. It is the underdeveloped Papua New Guinea,

---

[12] On Tibet, see Iyer (1989, p. 71).

11

divided by treacherous mountain ranges, that contains more than a quarter of the world's languages.[13]

Just as the mobility of people can have a homogenizing effect, so can the mobility of goods. Movie producers know that action films are easiest to export to many different countries. Heroism, excitement, and violence do not vary so much across cultures. Comedies, with their nuances of dialogue and their culturally specific references, are the hardest to sell abroad. A global market in cinema therefore encourages action films more than it does sophisticated comedy. Comedies for the global market tend to emphasize physical slapstick rather than clever wordplay, which is hard to translate into other languages. Some very fine movies use action and slapstick comedy, but these trends have not elevated the quality of movies in all regards.

## What Is to Come

Many writers address cross-cultural exchange from the perspectives of "critical theory." They draw upon a diverse set of approaches—including Marxism, structuralism, the Frankfurt School, and postmodernism—to provide a critique of capitalism and globalization. They view markets as promoting hegemony, alienation, and a dumbing down of taste. To varying degrees, Bourdieu, Gramsci, Habermas, and Canclíni all explore different aspects of these traditions. These thinkers cannot be reduced to a single common denominator, as is appropriate for such diverse (and global) intellectual products. Nonetheless they share common sources, taken largely from Continental philosophy, share a skepticism about market-driven culture, and have been influenced by Marxian economics.

In contrast to these sources, I use a "gains from trade" model to understand cultural exchange. Individuals who engage in cross-cultural exchange expect those transactions to make them better off, to enrich their cultural lives, and to increase their menu of choice.

---

[13] See "Cultural Loss Seen as Languages Fade."

Just as trade typically makes countries richer in material terms, it tends to make them culturally richer as well. Any story about the problems of globalization—and several plausible candidates will arise—must explain why this basic gains-from-trade mechanism might backfire.[14]

Chapter 2 examines the gains-from-trade story in more detail, showing how wealth, technology, and cross-cultural exchange drive many cultural blossomings. The following three chapters then consider three mechanisms that may overturn the gains-from-trade argument. Trade affects societal ethos and worldview, geographically clusters production of some goods and services, and alters customer thoughtfulness and concern for quality, not always for the better. These three mechanisms provide linchpins of anti-market arguments and thus they receive special attention.

I translate criticisms of globalization into stories about how individual cultural choices, made in the context of imperfect markets, may lead to undesirable consequences. In each case I examine how trade might damage creativity, convert anti-globalization polemics into a more systematic argument, and then assess the validity of the charges by looking at the evidence. When choosing empirical examples, I pay special attention to areas where the critics of globalization have been most vocal, such as cinema and handwoven textiles.

I do not seek to promote any single definition of what "quality" in global culture might consist of. One virtue of a broad menu of choice is to economize on the need for unanimity of opinion, which is hard to achieve. When it comes to the actual examples of quality culture, however, I have followed two principles. First, I have focused on what the critics cite as the hard cases for the optimistic perspective, as mentioned above. Second, when citing successes I have picked artistic creations that command widespread critical and popular support. For instance, I refer to French cooking, Persian car-

---

[14] In this regard my analysis differs from some of the writers who have defended synthetic or cosmopolitan culture. A variety of writers in the social sciences, such as James Clifford, Frederick Buell, Ulf Hannerz, Arjun Appadurai, and Edward Said, have pointed out the hybrid and synthetic nature of culture, but they have not focused on how the economics of trade shape that culture.

pets, and reggae music as examples of general cultural successes, though without meaning to endorse each and every manifestation of these genres. I do not spend time defending such judgments in aesthetic terms, which I take as given. Instead I focus on the role of the market, and cross-cultural exchange, in promoting or discouraging the relevant creations.

At the end of the day the reader must ultimately take home his or her personal opinion about whether a particular example is one of rot or one of cultural blossoming. I do not expect many readers to agree that every cited success is in fact splendid, but I hope nonetheless that the overall picture—which emphasizes the diversity of the menu of choice—will be a persuasive one.[15]

A discussion of globalization must range far and wide across numerous topics. Given my background as an economist, I approach each topic differently than might a specialist in a particular area. I have studied the relevant scholarly literature in each case, but the core of my knowledge results from my diverse experiences as a cultural consumer, rather than from a single path of specialized study. In the language of chapter 5, the book will sample topics extensively rather than intensively, and should be judged as such. Specialization, while it has brought immense benefits to science and academic life, is by its nature ill-suited to illuminate the diverse production and consumption made possible by the market economy.

The results of this inquiry will suggest three primary lessons, to be developed in the following chapters:

*The concept of cultural diversity has multiple and sometimes divergent meanings.*

It is misleading to speak of diversity as a single concept, as societies exhibit many kinds of diversity. For instance, diversity *within* society refers to the richness of the menu of choice in that society.

---

[15] An earlier book of mine, Cowen (1998), discusses aesthetic issues in more depth; I refer the interested reader to this treatment, especially chapter 5. In the literature I have found Hume (1985 [1777]), Herrnstein Smith (1988), Danto (1981), Savile (1982), and Mukarovsky (1970) to be especially enlightening.

Many critics of globalization, however, focus on diversity *across* societies. This concept refers to whether each society offers the same menu, and whether societies are becoming more similar.

These two kinds of diversity often move in opposite directions. When one society trades a new artwork to another society, diversity within society goes up (consumers have greater choice), but diversity across the two societies goes down (the two societies become more alike). The question is not about more or less diversity per se, but rather what kind of diversity globalization will bring. Cross-cultural exchange tends to favor diversity within society, but to disfavor diversity across societies.[16]

Note that diversity across societies is to some extent a collectivist concept. The metric compares one society to another, or one country to another, instead of comparing one individual to another, or instead of looking at the choices faced by an individual.

Critics of globalization commonly associate diversity with the notion of cultural differentiation across geographic space. In reality, individuals can pursue diverse paths without having their destinies determined by their place of origin; indeed this is central to the notion of freedom. But many proponents of diversity expect that differentiation should be visible to the naked eye, such as when we cross the border between the United States and Mexico. By comparing the collectives and the aggregates, and by emphasizing the dimension of geographic space, this standard begs the question as to which kind of diversity matters. Under an alternative notion of diversity, different regions may look more similar than in times past, but the individuals in those locales will have greater scope to pursue different paths for their lives, and will have a more diverse menu of choice for their cultural consumption.

Trade tends to increase *diversity over time* by accelerating the pace of change and bringing new cultural goods with each era or generation. If diversity is a value more generally, surely we have

---

[16] Weitzman (1992, 1993) develops an economic metric for diversity, but considers only differences across societies (or biological units), not the menu of choice within or the other concepts presented below.

some grounds for believing that diversity-over-time is a value as well. Yet many defenders of diversity decry the passing of previous cultures and implicitly oppose diversity-over-time. In the last chapter I will examine why this might be the case.

*Operative diversity*—how effectively we can enjoy the diversity of the world—differs from *objective diversity,* or how much diversity is out there. In some ways the world was very diverse in 1450, but not in a way that most individuals could benefit from. Markets have subsequently disseminated the diverse products of the world very effectively, even when those same cross-cultural contacts have damaged indigenous creative environments.

*Cultural homogenization and heterogenization are not alternatives or substitutes; rather, they tend to come together.*

Market growth causes heterogenizing and homogenizing mechanisms to operate in tandem. Some parts of the market become more alike, while other parts of the market become more different. Mass culture and niche culture are complements, once we take the broader picture into account. Growing diversity brings us more of many different things, which includes more mass culture as well.

Product differentiation and niche markets rely on certain kinds of social homogeneity. Mass marketing, for instance, also creates the infrastructure to peddle niche products to smaller numbers of consumers. Magazine advertising, mail order, and the Internet allow recording companies to make a profit issuing CDs that sell only five hundred copies. Book superstores enable readers to stumble across the products of small presses. Most generally, partial homogenization often creates the conditions necessary for diversity to flower on the micro level. Claude Lévi-Strauss noted, "Diversity is less a function of the isolation of groups than of the relationships which unite them."[17]

---

[17] Lévi-Strauss (1976, p. 328). Late-nineteenth-century sociology was strongly concerned with processes of differentiation and homogenization; see the works of Pareto and Weber. Shils (1981) is one twentieth-century work in this tradition.

Food markets illustrate the connection between heterogenization and homogenization with special clarity. Chain restaurants take
an increasing percentage of American and global restaurant sales,
and in this regard the market brings greater homogeneity. At the
same time, the growth in dining out has led to an expansion of food
opportunities of all kinds, whether it be fast food, foie gras, or Thai
mee krob. American suburbs and cities offer a wide variety of
Asian, Latin, African, and European foods, as well as "fusion" cuisines. High and low food-culture have proven to be complements,
not opposing forces. Paris and Hong Kong, both centers of haute
cuisine, have the world's two busiest Pizza Hut outlets.[18]

*Finally, cross-cultural exchange, while it will alter and disrupt each
society it touches, will support innovation and creative human energies.*

Cross-cultural exchange brings value clashes that cannot be re-
solved scientifically, as I will stress in the last chapter. So no investi-
gation, no matter how comprehensive, can provide a final evaluation of cultural globalization. The world as a whole has a broader
menu of choice, but older synthetic cultures must give way to newer
synthetic cultures. Countries will share more common products
than before. Some regions, in return for receiving access to the
world's cultural treasures, and the ability to market their products
abroad, will lose their distinctiveness. Not everyone likes these basic
facts.

These trade-offs aside, much of the skepticism about cross-cultural exchange has nothing to do with diversity per se. Most critics
of contemporary culture dislike particular trends, often those associated with modernity or commercialism more generally. They use diversity as a code word for a more particularist agenda, often of an
anti-commercial or anti-American nature. They care more about the
particular form that diversity takes in their favored culture, rather

---

[18] Pillsbury (1998, p. 183). On Pizza Hut, see *Harper's*, November 1994, p. 11. On
the growth in global food diversity, through trade, see Sokolov (1991).

than about diversity more generally, freedom of choice, or a broad menu of quality options.

In response to commonly pessimistic attitudes, I will outline a more optimistic and more cosmopolitan view of cross-cultural exchange. The "creative destruction" of the market is, in surprising ways, *artistic* in the most literal sense. It creates a plethora of innovative and high-quality creations in many different genres, styles, and media. Furthermore, the evidence strongly suggests that cross-cultural exchange expands the menu of choice, at least provided that trade and markets are allowed to flourish.[19]

Nonetheless, an informed cosmopolitanism must be of the cautious variety, rather than based on superficial pro-globalization slogans or cheerleading about the brotherhood of mankind. Throughout the book we will see that individuals are often more creative when they do not hold consistently cosmopolitan attitudes. A certain amount of cultural particularism and indeed provincialism, among both producers and consumers, can be good for the arts. The meliorative powers of globalization rely on underlying particularist and anti-liberal attitudes to some extent. Theoretically "correct" attitudes do not necessarily maximize creativity, suggesting that a cosmopolitan culture does best when cosmopolitanism itself is not fully believed or enshrined in social consciousness.

---

[19] I am indebted to John Tomasi for some of the wording of this paragraph, without wishing to hold him responsible for its use.

# 2
■ Global Culture Ascendant:
The Roles of Wealth and Technology

The economic case for trade provides a natural base for a cosmopolitan perspective on culture. Both art consumers and art producers need "otherness" to fulfill their creative wishes. Gains from trade arise when demanders and suppliers come together in markets, each bringing something different, to find a common interest in exchange. The very notion of exchange suggests a difference in initial endowments or desires, which of course may include cultural differences.

Technology and wealth, two prominent features of today's global markets, help drive these multicultural trade relationships. On the supply side, technology gives artists new ways of turning creative visions into marketable products. The printing press, the motion picture camera, acrylic paints, and the electric guitar, among many other modern technologies, benefit the arts around the world. "Low tech" innovations, including the metal carving knife, machine-made yarn for weaving, and the acoustic guitar, are no less important.

On the demand side, wealth creates the buying power to fund niche creations. Western customers have supported vital art forms in many poorer countries, whether it be the voodoo art of Haiti, the reggae music of Jamaica, or the paintings of the Australian Aborigines. A large and wealthy global market gives creators of many different kinds the opportunity to support themselves through selling their works.

Most generally, technology and wealth support the evolution of *art networks*, typically in conjunction with other social institutions, such as families, religions, and customary practices. The notion of art networks refers to the reliance of large-scale creative achievements on a complex combination of favorable circumstances. When a fruitful artistic era comes about, complementary pieces of the social fabric have accreted and meshed over time, until the appropriate environment is in place. In a more narrowly economic context, Ludwig Lachmann coined the term "capital complementarity" to refer to capital goods that increase each other's value. In highly creative epochs, a society's ethos, material technologies, and marketplace conditions all work together in cumulative fashion to create and support networks of productive artists.

It is well recognized that technology brings a broader menu of choice to world consumers, such as when individuals start watching television, listening to the radio, or visiting the local Walmart. Working from the gains from trade model, I focus instead on how technology and wealth stimulate innovative cultural *production* in the less economically developed countries. Technology, in addition to boosting the menu of choice within a society, often makes each society a richer source of creative energy as well.

Many poorer cultures are fragile with respect to technology, as the next chapter will discuss, and as many critics of globalization have charged. When the whole of a culture is greater than the sum of the parts, the whole may suffer if any one of the parts is pulled away. The nature of complementarity implies that each piece relies on the other pieces. The cautionary implications of this fact should not be neglected.

This chapter, however, focuses on the upside of complementarity. The same logic that accounts for the fragility of a culture also shows how and why a culture can become so dynamic. Complementarity implies that a culture can respond positively to new ideas and technologies, often in explosive fashion. Adding a single piece to the puzzle can make all the other pieces far more valuable. Foreign cultures commonly adapt new ideas and technologies in ways that their trading partners had never anticipated, which is precisely the theme of this chapter.

## ▬ Cities, and the Music of Zaire

Many cultural networks have blossomed in cities, from antiquity to the Italian Renaissance to Paris to the Chinese, Arabic, and pre-Hispanic civilizations of times past. Cities bring together buyers, mix cultural influences, and support thick, competitive networks of supply and training. Cities agglomerate resources in the service of highly specialized contributions to the arts.

Many of today's poorer countries have developed very large cities, usually through accident and migration rather than through conscious design. These cities, whatever their impracticalities and social costs, have become breeding grounds for new creative contributions to music, literature, cinema, and the visual arts. They have brought together diverse ethnic groups, often from rural areas, ideas and technologies from the wealthier countries, and middle-class and wealthy consumers, often in the guise of migrants or tourists. The modern city, of course, depends on transportation, electrification, and trade with the outside world.

The musics of Zaire (now Democratic Republic of the Congo) provide one example of how cities spur culture by attracting and combining foreign influences. If Africa has had any dominant postwar music, it is the dance music of Zaire. These musicians combine, in the words of one commentator, "a skipping snare drum beat, tight, sweet harmony choruses behind a light, mellifluous lead voice and, above all, the famous multiple intermeshed guitar lines."[1]

---

[1] See Sweeney (1991, p. 49). G. Stewart (2000) provides the definitive history of popular music in Zaire.

These musics were not indigenous tribal products but, rather, have relied on mining wealth, resource mobility, and electrification. The roots of Zairean popular music can be traced back to the 1920s, when work camps, mining towns, railroad companies, and military service brought together members of many diverse tribes for the first time. Other workers came from central Africa, Nigeria, Ivory Coast, the Cameroons, Mozambique, Malawi, as well as the West Indies, China, and Macau. Most of all, this mixing took place in the emerging modern cities, both in Zaire and in the directly adjacent Congo. In particular, Leopoldville (now Kinshasa) and Brazzaville became centers of detribalization and acculturation. While Zaire has since fallen apart, throughout most of this century it has been one of the richest parts of Africa, largely because of mining wealth.[2]

African, Western, and Caribbean influences mingled in this environment. Creative artists drew styles and rhythms from the spectrum of cultures converging in Zaire at that time. The emerging trade language, Lingala, served as the primary linguistic medium for the new Zairean musics. Entertainers experimented with thumb-pianos, drums, and bottle percussion, common instruments in African music at the time. The acoustic and later the electric guitar became prominent, as did the saxophone, trumpet, clarinet, and flute, none of which are indigenous to Africa.[3] Cuban influences, especially the Son, Mambo, Cha-Cha, Biguine, and Bolero, entered Zaire by the time of the Second World War. The process accelerated in the 1950s, when radio and cruise ships gave Cuban styles further exposure throughout East and Central Africa. Seventy-eight-rpm phonograph records of Cuban music were played in Zaire, often by hand-cranking in the absence of electricity. American rhythm and blues music, brought by the same media, became a prominent influence as well. Immigrants from Greece set up many of the recording studios for Zairean musical stars.[4]

[2] On urbanization and mixing, see Bokelenge (1986), Kazadi (1973), Mukuna (1979–80), Mukuna (1980), and Almquist (1993, p. 75).

[3] See Barlow and Eyre (1995, p. 26).

[4] On the transmission of Cuban music to Africa, see Mensah (1980, p. 187), Santoro (1993), and Ewens (1991, pp. 56, 129). Botombele (1976, pp. 32–33) and G. Stew-

By the postwar era, Zaire had emerged as the music capital of Africa. Open-air "Congo-bars" became commonplace in Kinshasa. Restaurants and cabarets for non-Africans began to hire Zairean musical ensembles for evening entertainment. The music quarter of Matonge bustled twenty-four hours a day. On the radio, the new popular Zairean styles replaced traditional African musics. By the mid-1950s, the battery-run transistor was widespread and served as the main means of disseminating music. In the late 1940s, several recording studios had been established; by 1955 they had released five thousand titles. This was the age of Wendo, Bosco, Malapet, Essous, Jhimmy, Franco and OK Jazz, and Joseph Kabaselle ("Le Grande Kalle"). The style known as "rumba" dates from this era. Zairean music developed export markets throughout Africa, selling strongly in West Africa and virtually sweeping Kenya, Uganda, and Tanzania, where the Zairean musical influence remains prevalent to this day.[5]

Zaire is but one example of broader trends. African nations, from Senegal to Ghana to South Africa, have been hotbeds of musical creativity since at least the Second World War. In each case cities proved to be a breeding ground for mixing Western and "native" influences, often of an originally tribal nature. The original ideas and inspirations of tribal groups have been commodified, and shaped into new synthetic forms, for the purpose of courting outside markets. The resulting products have won both commercial success and critical plaudits.

More generally, the economically poorer nations have used Western technologies and the modern city to drive a host of innovations in fields as diverse as literature, cinema, and the visual arts. African cinema draws heavily on tribal storytelling traditions, and is more narrative than most Western movies, while retaining many of the advantages of the cinematic medium. Third World artists

---

art (2000) discuss influences on Zairean music more generally. On the transistor, see Harrev (1989, p. 109). On the role of Greeks, see G. Stewart (2000).

[5] See Kazadi (1971), Graham (1985), Almquist (1993, p. 75), Barlow and Eyre (1995, pp. 26–27), Wallis and Malm (1984, p. 32), and Roberts (1972, chap. 9).

have used acrylic paints, oil paints, and modern sculptural materials to bring their native inspirations to new audiences. The fiction of India combines sources such diverse sources as Dickens, the Koran, and the Indian religious epic, again relying on modern Western institutions to mobilize the writer's inspiration into a commercially viable product.

## ■ The New World Cultural Explosion

The twentieth century brought a cultural explosion to most of the New World, not just to the United States and Canada. Mexico, Brazil, Cuba, and Haiti, among other locales, moved from being cultural backwaters to vibrant creative centers with global influence and acclaim.

New World creativity typically has been both synthetic and commercial in nature. The Kuna Indians, who live on the San Blas Islands off the eastern coast of Panama, put Western technologies and materials to unexpected uses. Prior to Western contact, the Kuna had a well-developed religion and cosmology, a strong and unique ethos, and native artistic traditions of body painting, but they lacked the suitable media for a full development of their creative powers.

The subsequent development of the Kuna arts has relied heavily on trade with wealthier regions. Today the *mola* arts are the most prominent Kuna cultural invention; mola means blouse in the Kuna Indian language but a mola more generally is a cut-cotton panel with a colorful design. The mola evolved during the nineteenth century, as a spin-off from painted cloth, which the Kuna learned in the eighteenth century, possibly from French Huguenots. European contact later brought manufactured cloth, metal sewing needles, and scissors, which made mola production possible. Since that time, mola makers have supported themselves by selling to tourists in Panama or cruise ships visiting the San Blas Islands.

The very topics of molas represent this multicultural heritage. Molas portray not only native life and pagan gods, but also soccer stars, Christian saints, the Panama Canal, cruise ships, helicopters, and spaceships, among other foreign subjects. The words and letters on the mola can be taken from lottery tickets, belt buckles, or cans of beans. Like their molas, the clothing of the Kuna is highly international. Their fabrics come from Colombia and China, their red and yellow cotton head scarves come from Japan, their necklace coins originate in Panama, Colombia, and the United States, and their trade beads are Czechoslovakian in origin.[6]

Since the end of the Second World War, the Caribbean has been one of the most creative and vital sources of world culture. Wealth and technology have enabled these countries to blend African, Latin, native Indian, Asian, European, and North American influences into a coherent whole.

The steel band ensembles of Trinidad acquired their instruments—fifty-gallon oil drums—from the multinational oil companies. Large numbers of these containers were brought to the island by the American armed forces during the Second World War, and abandoned when the war was over. At first Trinidad steel band musicians played on biscuit tins, paint and zinc cans, metal tins from abattoirs, frying pans, soda drums, car wheel rims, and automobile chassis, as they experimented in the slum yards of the Port of Spain. Once these metallic options became available, the "indigenous" percussion technology of bamboo was abandoned. Bamboo instruments could not produce the same variety of sounds and had a much shorter life-span, due to their limited ability to withstand constant percussive pounding. The first all-metal bands were active in the late 1930s.

Technological improvements have been frequent since the early days of the art. Metallic instruments were fully refined only when the superior sound of the oil drum was discovered. Steel band musicians learned how to strike a variety of drums of different sizes, shapes, and alloys. They cut off the head of the drum and created a

---

[6] See Kapp (1972, p. 10), Salvador (1976, p. 171), Mathews (1998, pp. 10–13), and Weatherford (1994, p. 197). On the Kuna more generally, see Puls (1988) and Howe (1998).

series of bumps on the surface, each corresponding to a desired musical note. Early steel drums were often out of tune, but as the pan-makers learned the laws of acoustics through experimentation, they refined pan construction into a science. The use of oil drums allowed for more notes to be tuned on a pan, higher-quality notes, and notes of longer sustenance and varied resonance. The steel band draws on the basic ideas of the xylophone orchestra (an early influence), while using the properties of metal to create a sound that is more shimmering and susceptible to greater variations in pitch and attack.[7]

The steel band has drawn upon other international influences as well, especially the Indian *tassa* drum ensemble. The form of the steel band ensemble, the relationship between lead and background players, the use of biscuit drums, and the way the pans are treated to alter pitch all were influenced by this Indian tradition. In the St. James neighborhood of Port of Spain, where the Indian and Muslim communities are prominent, the various musical traditions intermingled and influenced each other.[8]

Ironically it is in Trinidad that Western classical music has survived best as a truly popular art. Steel bands play many kinds of music, from Western pop tunes to original compositions, but the classics have remained consistently popular. Steel bands have succeeded with their renditions of melodies by Bach, Mozart, Handel, Strauss, Tchaikovsky, and others. Some Trinidadians have criticized the steel bands for playing European music, but the bands have ignored these criticisms, seeking to attract as many listeners as possible.

Dub has been one of the most influential forms of Jamaican music, forming a base for today's electronica, techno, and rave movements. Dub, an offshoot of reggae, was an early form of instrumental electronic music pioneered by King Tubby in the early 1970s. The dub movement took the reggae sound—the multitrack re-

---

[7] On the advantages of the oil drums, see Stuempfle (1995, p. 41). On the development of metal, and oil drums more specifically, see Nunley (1996, pp. 133–36). On the xylophone influence, see Stuempfle (1995, pp. 248–49n).

[8] See Stuempfle (1995, p. 40).

cording studio, echoes, and overdubs—to its logical conclusion. Jamaican dub producers literally deconstruct reggae songs, breaking them down into their constituent parts, emphasizing the instrumental parts, slowing down the tempi, spreading the sounds out with echoes, and altering the rhythms. At first dub cuts were B-side instrumental remixes of A-side reggae singles; since the A-side usually sells the single, musicians could take chances with the B-side. Shortly thereafter, full-scale dub albums were released. For those convinced that technology will defeat local cultures, ask who, thirty-five years ago, would have expected a small Caribbean island to become a world leader in experimental electronic music?[9]

Caribbean music shows the importance of technology more generally. Technologies of transportation and electronic reproduction allow Third World and indigenous artists to market their products to Western consumers.

Successful Jamaican musicians sell to relatively wealthy audiences abroad, especially in the United States and the United Kingdom. By the end of the 1960s, the U.K. was the largest single market for Jamaican releases, and the United States has taken on growing importance with time. The genre of reggae is best known, but Jamaicans also have produced mento, ska, rocksteady, rasta, ragga, dub, dance hall, and lovers' rock, among other forms. Kingston is dotted with hundreds of recording studios, and Jamaica has more record labels than does the United Kingdom.[10]

[9] On the roots of reggae, and various Jamaican styles, see Hebdige (1990) and Bergman (1985, chap. 1).

[10] On the U.K. market, see Bradley (1996, p. 101). Although Jamaica is a relatively small nation of less than three million people, Jamaican styles have exerted great influence on American and English music. Paul McCartney ("C Moon"), The Clash (any), Blondie ("The Tide is High"), The Police, and Paul Simon ("Mother and Child Reunion") all have drawn on reggae. Much of the impetus behind American rap came from Jamaican "toasting" music. Reggae also is a powerful influence in the musics of Africa and of other Caribbean nations. Jamaican DJ influences became prominent in the late 1970s and 1980s, as DJs added their own commentary to the records they played from the sound systems. Many early rappers came from Jamaica and adapted this style for the American market. Kool Herc had come to the South Bronx from Kingston and took his style from Jamaican DJs. Rappers also were influenced by the reggae practice of "toasting," a DJ style that offers a half-sung, half-shouted vocal accompaniment to a rough beat. See Costello and Wallace (1990).

The 1950s, arguably the most vital period of Cuban music, coincided with Cuba's greatest openness to the outside world. The Cuba of this era was a relatively wealthy nation by Caribbean standards, second in Latin America only to Argentina. Cuban cities had department stores, five and dimes, modern supermarkets, ice cream parlors, American cars, and first-run American movies, all in relatively large numbers. This era brought the Cuban musical tradition to its peak, through such stars as Celia Cruz, Beny Moré, Cachao, Pérez Prado, the Trio Matamoros, the septet of Ignacio Piñeiro, the Orquesta Aragón, Guillermo Portabales, and the Sonora Matancera. The recent best-selling CD *Buena Vista Social Club* draws heavily on performers from this older Cuban generation of musicians.

Cuba developed such an advanced musical network in part because it was so "Americanized." Capitalist wealth financed the big bands, dance clubs, and concert halls that created the new Cuban sounds. American tourists, who in those days went to Cuba in great numbers, were avid supporters of Cuban music. Cuban recordings were commonly issued in the United States.

The Cuban mass media popularized this musical explosion to the native Cuban audience as well. Nearly 90 percent of Cuban homes had radios, and Cuba had over two-hundred thousand televisions, ninth in the world despite her small population. These media financed Cuban performers and promoted them to relatively large audiences. Furthermore, Cuba's accessible location and media culture allowed its musicians to draw upon Spanish, North American, and African influences.[11]

The financial success of Cuban music relied also on Cuban cultural imperialism and the export of music by modern technology. The international Latin music known as salsa is based in Cuban

---

[11] On the role of Cuban mass media, see Manuel (1988, p. 33). The initially favorable cultural mix helped as well. Cuban music has an especially strong connection with Africa. Although slavery had been abolished elsewhere, large numbers of slaves were imported as late as the 1870s in Cuba (and as late as the 1880s in Brazil). African influences continued to feed into Cuban music relatively late in its development, increasing its rhythmic complexity and emotional power. This African connection provided the base for subsequent Cuban musicians to build on.

dance music, and Cuban influences have strongly shaped the musical cultures of Puerto Rico and the Dominican Republic. Haitian compas music has strongly Cuban roots. Cuban music has been a dominant influence in East and Central Africa throughout much of the twentieth century, as discussed above. Cuba used these markets to finance and refine its native musical styles.[12]

The matching of rich buyers to poor creators also has helped the visual arts flourish. Early Haitian visual styles drew on African and voodoo roots, but other foreign influences have been significant. Haitian paintings show uncanny resemblances with early French folk and Naive art, and we can only wonder what connections existed.

Haitian painting had no significant world presence until 1943, when the U.S. government assigned DeWitt Peters, an American watercolor painter, to teach English in Port-au-Prince. Peters was surprised that Haiti did not have a single art gallery. Peters set up an arts center (Centre d'Art) to encourage native Haitian creativity. Hector Hyppolite, the most renowned Haitian painter, started his art career early in the century by drawing "postcards" for the occupying U.S. Marines. He later painted homes and signs and decorated furniture. He was discovered by Peters in 1943, when Peters saw a painted wineshop door by Hyppolite in a small village north of Port-au-Prince. In 1944 Peters bought a painting from Philomé Obin and sent him supplies to ease his financial burdens; Obin also became one of the leading Haitian painters. Obin had been a bookkeeper in Cap Haitian but then turned his attention to art. Rigaud

---

[12] Ironically, several policies of the Castro regime have protected the quality of these capitalistic musical forms. (Some) musicians are among the few professionals allowed to work as private entrepreneurs and keep their earnings. Music is thus a relatively profitable avocation and it continues to enjoy high status. With the assistance of the American embargo, Cuban communism has limited economic growth and kept much of the earlier cultural ethos intact. Cuba feels like a time capsule into the past, with its old automobiles and Art Deco architecture. The lack of globalization has limited progress, but also has prevented earlier Cuban musical styles from being corrupted, or from selling out to the American mass market. Cuban music (though not the Cuban people) therefore has had the best of two worlds. Globalization set it in motion, but now relative isolation protects it from homogenizing trends. Cuba continues to enjoy one of the world's richest musical cultures, although the economy is a failure more generally.

Benoit, a taxi driver, approached Peters with his painted terra-cotta pots and received support as well, later becoming one of the most renowned Haitian artists. Préfète Dufaut started by drawing geometric murals on the walls of his hut. He developed his style only after receiving paints from an American journalist living in Haiti at the time.[13]

Since that time, Haitian Naive art has been funded and publicized by a largely foreign clientele of Europeans and Americans. Most of the leading early Haitian painters received their initial encouragement, financial support, or artistic materials from American tourists, visitors, or residents. American writer Selden Rodman helped plan, organize, and finance the large painted murals at the cathedral Sainte Trinité in Port-au-Prince, usually considered the high point of Haitian artistic achievement. The completion of the cathedral relied on a grant from American philanthropist Mrs. Vincent Astor.[14]

Other voodoo arts, such as the dolls and "mojo boards" of Pierrot Barra, use abandoned American toys and dolls, scavenged by "runners" from the garbage dumps of Port-au-Prince. Barra and other voodoo artists also use mirrors, sequins, satins, and parts of used cars. Haitian voodoo flags, now the hot artistic form in Haiti, took their initial designs taken from eighteenth-century French military banners. Sequins later became prominent in the flags, and they were taken originally from an abandoned American sequin factory. Antoine Oleyant, commonly considered the best voodoo flag-maker, relied on the early support of Richard Morse, a half-American, half-Haitian rock star, who owns the Hotel Olafsson and gave Antoine studio space there.

Morse also helped the island develop its musical culture. Morse's band Ram has released successful recordings and has

---

[13] Rodman (1948, pp. 4–9). On postcards, see Rodman (1988, p. 49). See Rodman (1948, p. 60) on Hyppolite's door, and Rodman (1988, p. 71) and Rodman (1961, p. 98).

[14] On the origins of Haitian painting, see Danticat and Demme (1997, pp. 23–24) and Rodman (1948). On Lam and Breton, see Rodman (1988, p. 49). On tourist buyers and the cathedral, see Rodman (1948, pp. 4–5, 9, 93) and Rodman (1982, p. 123) on

helped stimulate interest in Haitian voodoo and rara music, the latter played with horns after the time of Carnival. Morse also helped Boukman Eskperyans, one of the leading Haitian bands, get started in the music business. This group pioneered the style of "voodoo beat," which reintroduced voodoo drums into recorded Haitian popular music. Rather than "corrupting" Haitian music, these groups have restored interest in some of its older traditions.[15]

Part of the genius of creation, no matter where we find it, comes in knowing when to borrow ideas or look for the assistance of others. The Haitian visual arts show the genius of the Haitians as synthesists, and this genius does not differ in kind from what we find in the richer countries.

## ■ Preserving and Extending Past Culture

Wealth and technology not only bring the new, they also help cultures preserve and extend the best of their past. Most artistic and musical products from the poorer nations were not made to be especially durable but, rather, were intended for the immediate moment. Lack of durability is common when wealth is low, technologies are few, and short-run survival is a pressing need. Western technologies, however, have enabled many cultural products to last and to reach wider audiences.

Musical notation—an essentially Western idea—has helped preserve many non-Western musics that would otherwise have disappeared or changed beyond recognition. Musicians and scholars in the Arab and Persian worlds have adopted notation with enthusiasm, knowing that their musics are in continual flux, even without Western influence. Compositions that would have perished with the death of a generation will now persist and will be accessible to future musicians.

---

Mrs. Astor. On early American support for leading Haitian painters, see Rodman (1988, pp. 49, 71; 1948, p. 60; and 1961, p. 98).

[15] On Morse, see Sweeney (1991, p. 214). The author has interviewed Morse as well.

Cheap cassette players have supported many traditional Third World musics by allowing artists to reach audiences at low cost. Profitable cassette production requires only a small circle of dedicated fans, sometimes as few as several hundred. In Indonesia the spread of the cassette, starting in the 1970s, supported traditional and popular musics that had been shut out by government-controlled radio. In India cassette music has revitalized local musical traditions. Entrepreneurs now produce cassette music played in regional styles and sung in regional dialects. The film music from Bombay and Madras, in contrast, serves mass taste and is sung primarily in the widely spoken languages, such as Hindi. Relative to radio, cassettes have helped decentralize the decision of whether or not to fund a music and thus have boosted artistic productivity.[16]

Technology often plays a hidden role in supporting indigenous creativity. Art forms that appear independent of modern technology in fact often rely on it.

Tuvan throat singers from Mongolia send vibrations from deep down the throat while singing. The effect is one of overtones, where the vocalist produces two notes at once without relying on any material technology. It is unknown how long the Tuvans have been singing in this fashion, but since the practice is shared by various Eskimo tribes, who are related to the Tuvans, it appears to be ancient in origin. At first glance this activity appears to be independent of material technology, but in reality recording and radio have provided critical support for throat singing in recent times. A group from the Smithsonian went into Tuvan territory and made a number of highly regarded and profitable recordings. Since the success of the recordings,

---

[16] On how cassettes have influenced Third World musics, see Manuel (1993), Hatch (1989), and Sutton (1985). While copyright problems have been rampant, the mainstream artists have been the greatest losers from unauthorized copying. The minority-culture products would not have found a large audience in the first place. Tapes, which can be conveniently carried, transported, or passed hand-to-hand, also allow music to bypass government censorship and control. The record industries, film industries, and radio stations of many developing countries are either controlled by government authorities or controlled by corporations with strong state connections. Cassette music bypasses these restraints.

younger Tuvans have shown greater interest in learning throat singing. Recording, by expanding the size of the market, has stimulated
Tuvan musical innovation as well as preservation of older styles. Recording, of course, is not the only significant technology in this example. The Tuvans benefited indirectly from the air travel, the antibi-
otics, and the sturdy walking shoes of the Western visitors. A recent
American movie on Tuvan throat singing, *Gengis Blues*, may expand
the popularity of the genre further.[17]

## ■ Can Wealthier Societies Afford the Arts?

Under one complaint, wealth is bad for many forms of the arts. Artists and artisans from the poorer countries supposedly give up their
creative endeavors once their society becomes rich and commercial-
izes. The logic here is easy to see: why, after all, work as a hand-
weaver for a dollar a day when a new local factory is offering twice
as much?[18]

In reality, economic growth usually leads to a reallocation of creative activity to the dynamic and growing artistic sectors, rather
than the death of the arts. The poorer countries in the world have
virtually exploded with creative art, music, and literature in the
twentieth century. All creative genres will decline, given enough
time, but the overall picture is dynamic and full of success stories.

Pessimistic critics sometimes focus too narrowly on a single aspect of the creative process. Traditional African drumming may in
due time decline, but it is being replaced by a variety of creative
African urban musics based on acoustic and electric guitars. Modern Indian architecture cannot match the Taj Mahal, but cinema,
music, cuisine, and design are blossoming there. The overall story

---

[17] See Weatherford (1994, pp. 252–53).

[18] The writings of William J. Baumol (with co-authors) provide one possible ratio-
nale for this pessimistic argument. Baumol's presentation of his "cost-disease" argument has evolved over time, but its early form predicted that economic growth
would cause the performing arts to shrink. See Cowen (1996, 1998), and Cowen and
Grier (1996), for a detailed examination of this argument.

is one of poor societies that develop new styles, methods, and genres as they become richer.

High wages pull creators out of a sector only when the production process of that sector is fixed and relies on simple human labor. These assumptions tend to hold for men's barbering, shoeshines, or prostitution. We often see more of these services in poorer countries than in richer ones, and perhaps the quality of service is higher in the poorer countries as well. But these assumptions do not provide a good model for most forms of creative artistic production. In reality most forms of creative activity rely on complex networks of innovation, production, and distribution. The more complex the network of production, the greater the number of potential ways that new technologies can be put to fruitful use, and the greater the likelihood that wealth and technology will bring creative booms.

## ▄▄ Textiles

Commercialism and markets have brought underappreciated benefits for handwoven textiles. Let us start with Persian textiles, arguably the most central and "classical" of the textile arts by Western standards. Next will follow a look at East Indian and American Indian textiles, supposedly two of the most difficult cases for markets and globalization.

### Persia

Persian weaving is ancient in origin, but the first Golden Age of Persian carpets came under the Safavid Empire (1499?–1722). During these years, Persia enjoyed political stability and prosperity. A rich variety of arts flourished, from calligraphy to Islamic miniatures to carpetweaving.

Persian carpets combined urban and rural cultures into a larger creative whole. Rural cultures brought basic technologies of weaving and design. Urban cultures refined these sources, improved the techniques, and drew design inspirations from illustrated manuscripts, ceramics, and painting. Mongol and Chinese traditions were especially important.[19] This urban-rural synthesis had crystallized by the end of the fifteenth century. By this time rug weaving ceased to be a purely nomadic folk art and moved into the urban commercial nexus.

Aggressive marketing enabled carpetmakers to recruit foreign buyers. European buyers were significant in the seventeenth and late sixteenth centuries, but until then most of the export trade was to the Ottoman Empire and India. Most of the Safavid carpets were aimed at the luxury end of the market, which partly accounts for their very high quality.[20]

Persian carpetmaking was in fact an aggressive form of cultural imperialism. Foreign carpetmakers were forced to adapt and improve their products to meet the Persian challenge, thus giving rise to many of the world's most accomplished carpetmaking traditions. Persian textiles revolutionized carpetmaking in adjoining areas, including in Turkestan, the Caucasus, and India (see further below). The Europeans also started to make knotted rugs as a result of contact with Persian products. Persian creations start to appear regularly in the paintings of van Dyck, Vermeer, Rubens, and Velázquez, among others. Many of these carpets reached Europe through the activities of Armenian merchants in the international silk trade.[21]

Starting in the last half of the seventeenth century, however, the quantity and quality of Persian textiles declined sharply. For complex historical reasons, the Persian state fell apart and international

[19] See Bennett (1996, p. 41), and Helfgott (1994, p. 53).

[20] Helfgott (1994) is the best general source on the rise of Persian carpetmaking. J. Thompson (1988) provides a good overview of workshop organization and of production at the luxury end of the market; see p. 152 on the latter. On the relatively small influence of the royal workshops, see Helfgott (1994, p. 53); see p. 55 on the growth of European buyers. At this time, foreign buyers played an even more significant role in Turkey. The Turkish production boom of the sixteenth and seventeenth centuries was driven largely by the possibility of exporting to European merchants and nobles. Many Turkish carpets from this era are called "Lottos" or "Holbeins," because they appear so frequently in paintings by Lorenzo Lotto or Hans Holbein. See J. Harris (1993, p. 120).

[21] Helfgott (1994, pp. 56–59, 63).

and regional trade networks for the carpets collapsed. By the nineteenth century, Persian carpetmaking was barely an active trade, and the finest of Persian carpets were no longer made.[22]

Persian carpets made a significant comeback in the nineteenth century, due largely to contact with the wealthier West. At this time European and North American buyers experienced a renewed love for the art, driven partly by new accumulations of industrial wealth.

The renaissance started when older Persian carpets were shown at international expositions in Europe and North America, starting with the 1873 World's Fair in Vienna. Carpet marketing spread to the West quickly, as American and European rug dealers imported textiles from Persia on a regular basis. High-quality department stores, such as Liberty in London, or W. J. Sloane in New York, carried Persian hand-knotted carpets for their buyers. In the rural parts of the United States, traveling dealers set up shows in hotel lobbies and furniture stores. The purchase of the now-famous Safavid "Ardebil" carpet by the South Kensington Museum (now the Victoria and Albert Museum) in 1892, for the then-unprecedented sum of £2,500, put a stamp of high-culture legitimacy on the field. By the time of the First World War, tens of thousands of buyers had entered the market.[23]

Tabriz merchants led the nineteenth-century boom, but the organization of production was no longer solely a Persian prerogative. European companies sent over representatives and became involved in the design and the expansion of workshops. Many of the Persian workshops were owned and run by European interests,

---

[22] See P. Baker (1995, p. 144), and Helfgott (1994, pp. 14, 72–79, 89). To cite a few developments, the invasion by Afghanistan in 1722 marked a nadir for Persia, but the underlying problems persisted until well into the nineteenth century. Bandits and corrupt government officials threatened the security of private property and made investment excessively risky. Seventeenth-century European mercantilist policies, which discouraged the importation of finished goods, hurt Persian carpetmaking as well. England and Holland cemented these policies through their growing control of trade through the Persian Gulf and the Indian Ocean. Eastern Europe nobles, an important source of demand for the Persian market, cut back their purchases due to their own economic troubles. The English also started buying textiles from India.

[23] See Helfgott (1994, pp. 15, 85–87).

such as the Ziegler workshops of Tabriz and Sultanabad, which were initiated in 1883 and expanded rapidly. Similarly, many Turkish textile workshops were run by British merchant houses.[24]

A very high percentage of extant Persian antique carpets date from this era. Western demand led to the reopening of old carpetmaking workshops and the establishment of new ones. In some areas, such as Shiraz, Abadeh, Hamadan, Nain, Isfahan, Sultanabad, and the Arak area, high-quality carpetmaking sprung up in areas that previously had only marginal carpetmaking traditions. The skills had been present in tribal and nomadic cultures, but outside purchasing power mobilized them towards more ambitious ends. By the end of the nineteenth century, hand-knotted rugs were Persia's largest export to the West and a source of Persian cultural pride.[25]

The same themes of trade and wealth show up in the history of textiles in nearby Caucasia. The Caucasus, a strategic corridor for the surrounding region, has been subject to powerful influences from Greek, Roman, Byzantine, Arab, Ottoman, Persian, Russian, and European civilizations. The small area contains more than fifty separate peoples and six major ethno-linguistic groups (Caucasians, Indo-Europeans, Mongols, Turks, Semites, and Finno-Ungrians). Rather than drawing on pure indigenous traditions, Caucasian carpetmaking has been an explicitly synthetic art from the beginning.[26]

The Caucasus produced beautiful carpets during the Safavid time in neighboring Persia, but its textile traditions did not expand to a significant level until the late nineteenth century. The Caucasus changed fundamentally when a railroad was built from Batoum to Tiflis in 1875. This development, along with other improvements in transportation, connected the Caucasus to the outside world. The foreign interest in Caucasus rugs stimulated weaving in the commercial centers and Caucasus rug production boomed. Caucasian

[24] On foreign-initiated workshops, see Milanesi (1993, p. 109), Helfgott (1994, pp. 141, 200, 213–17), Baker (1995, p. 144), Owen (1981, p. 212), and Edwards (1960, pp. 135–36).

[25] On the new traditions, see Helfgott (1994, p. 136).

[26] See Cootner (1981, p. 91).

production was a rural cottage industry, rather than based in urban workshops, but over time the skills of the smaller cottage industries were brought to larger factories. The 1880s served as a watershed period for Caucasian rugs, and most high-quality Caucasian rugs were produced between 1880 and 1920. In the golden age of Caucasian rugs, most of them were made for export, usually to the Western world.[27]

In terms of influences, the Caucasus drew heavily on the earlier Islamic textile traditions, working mostly from modifications of Persian designs and from nomadic folk art. Chinese designs and products were a source of ideas as well. Other sources were more eclectic. Caucasian weavers drew from Moscow chintz and from the designs on cheap wallpaper. The paper used to wrap toilet soap was another common source of design inspiration. Just as they have drawn on a wide variety of sources, Caucasus rugs have exerted broad international influence. The styles of beadwork on Sioux bags, for instance, are believed to have been influenced strongly by the designs on Caucasian rugs carried by the American settlers moving westward.[28]

### Handweaving: Gandhi and Textiles

Western technology has supported cultural networks in Third World and indigenous societies even in many sectors where it has a bad name. Cultural globalization, for instance, has an especially negative reputation in the area of handwoven textiles. According to standard accounts, machine-made products have driven handweavers out of business.

This charge has been especially pronounced in the context of East India. The standard view has been expressed by Satish Kumar: "[The] basis [of the Indian economy] had traditionally been in textiles. Each village had its spinners, carders, dyers, and weavers who were the heart of the village economy. However, when India was

[27] See Cootner (1981, pp. 91–93), and Helfgott (1994, p. 88); on the absence of the urban workshop, see J. Thompson (1988, p. 106).

[28] On Caucasian sources, see Wright and Wertime (1995, p. 43). On Caucasian influence, see Dubin (1987, pp. 262, 289). Other Sioux sources were European embroidery, needlepoint, and lacework.

flooded with machine-made, inexpensive, mass-produced textiles from Lancashire, the local textile artists were rapidly put out of business, and the village economy suffered terribly." Gandhi was especially vituperative in his campaign against foreign cloth, which he described as "filthy," "defiling," "untouchable," and "our greatest outward pollution." His *Swadeshi* movement suggested that Indians burn their foreign clothes, even if they were on the verge of subsistence. This historical example, probably more than any other, has been cited as an example of how globalized technologies destroy native cultures. Ironically, the Western movie *Gandhi* (itself a globalized product) has been partially responsible for spreading this myth.[29]

In reality, modern technologies have done more to boost Indian handweaving than to destroy it. Handweaving, although it no longer accounts for the entire Indian textile market, nonetheless has risen in absolute terms. Mechanization, by lowering the price of cloth, caused the absolute size of the market to expand greatly, which has supported more handweaving. The aesthetic craft of handweaving benefited from machine technologies, even though the incomes of many handweavers fell.

Western technologies provided critical pieces of the economic network behind Indian handweaving. The railroad, introduced by the British, made it possible for handweavers to sell to larger regional and national markets, and away from repetitious hand labor. The linking of cloth markets gave handweavers access to new and extensive networks of middlemen, and moved handweavers towards new and efficient means of larger-scale organization. The railway also brought cheap and high-quality foreign yarns to handweavers, which increased the quantity and quality of their output. Since the nineteenth century, most Indian folk weaving has relied

---

[29] The quotation is from Kumar (1996, p. 422). On Gandhi, see Tarlo (1996, p. 92). B. Chandra (1968) produces a more scholarly statement of the case against British market-penetration, although he adduces no statistical evidence that Indian handweaving declined; more on this below. Note that the word India, in this context, refers to "historic India," and thus includes modern-day Pakistan, unless otherwise stated.

on mill-made yarn, a product of Western influence, rather than on hand-made yarn. In addition to lowering costs, mill-made yarn allows creative human effort to be redirected to pattern design and composition, rather than mere repetitious labor.[30]

The major beneficiaries of the Swadeshi movement seem to have been Indian mills (who gave some funding to the movement), not handweavers. By targeting all foreign goods, Swadeshi, to the extent it was effective, denied useful foreign yarns to domestic hand-weavers.[31]

Handwoven Indian textiles remain aesthetically vibrant to this day. The domestic Indian demand for traditional, handwoven tex-tiles is based in the quality of the product. India is an extremely diverse nation, and most of its communities continue to express de-mands for very particular forms of quality textile production. These demands are rooted in marriage ceremonies, religious rituals, and local festivals. Handwoven textiles have consistently outperformed machine-made products for supplying these sectors, whether in the nineteenth century or today. The local handweavers still market spe-cialized textile products with success, given their greater knowledge of local customs and the rapidly shifting calendar of festivals. Saris, silk brocades, and other forms of quality weave and clothing con-tinue to support handweaving as well. Indian women in the north-west, especially the states of Gujarat and Rajastan, as well as in Paki-stan, are among the world's foremost practitioners of folk embroidery. Note that India accounts for almost a quarter of the world's population and a much higher percentage of its handweav-ing, so this experience represents a significant portion of the total global story for handweaving.[32]

While the data are limited, they do not support Gandhi's view of a decline in handweaving. Today India alone has over three mil-lion handlooms and six million weavers. Given that the active labor

---

[30] On these points, see Mehta (1953, p. 95), and also Anstey (1936, pp. 222–23).

[31] On Swadeshi, see Bagchi (1972, p. 224).

[32] On marketing advantages, see C. Baker (1984, p. 397). More generally, see Coo-per and Gillow (1996, p. 90). Barnard (1993, p. 133) provides another brief description of the vitality of the textile arts in contemporary India. Lynton (1995) surveys the sari tradition.

force in 1800 was about fifty to sixty million, handweaving is unlikely to have comprised ten percent of the total labor force in that period. Throughout the twentieth century, the available measures of handweaving suggest an absolute increase. At the beginning of World War I, hand looms were using 10 to 12 percent more yarn than two decades earlier. A measurement from 1936 to 1939 indicates that the yarn available to hand looms was nearly 37 percent more than from 1906 to 1909, even though the world was in the midst of a significant depression. Another estimate, comparing 1914 to 1934, found that hand looms had increased by 38 percent over that period. Even in Bombay, the center of Indian factory-cotton manufacture, the number of hand looms rose by 15 percent over this period.[33]

Insofar as machines did put some hand looms out of business, this did not necessarily damage product quality. Many handwoven Indian textile products had been of very low quality, using simple colors, coarse materials, and crudely uneven patterns. Today handweaving implies a higher-quality textile product only *because* mill-made products took over the lower-quality end of the market. Furthermore, competition with British factories and modern technologies forced Indian textile producers to make finer and more elaborate designs. The Indian weavers needed to offer their consumers a commodity that could not be replicated by machine. This spurred improvements in the quality of Indian textiles, as handweavers focused their attention on finer grades of production and design.[34]

The Indian experience with handweaving is not unique in this regard. In Egypt and the Middle East, handweavers survived by

[33] On the number of hand looms and workers, see Lynton (1995, p. 12). On the older figures, see Morris (1983, pp. 669–70), Bagchi (1972, pp. 220–28, 245), and Buchanan (1934, p. 214). Morris (1969, p. 160) estimates the number of eighteenth-century handweavers. Borpujari (1973), who focuses on the "cotton famines" of the 1860s, also stresses the resilience of Indian handweavers relative to the British. See also Farnie (1979, p. 99): "The crisis of their trade seems to have been only local and temporary and to have been followed by a renaissance as they responded to the challenge of alien competition." Even the relatively skeptical estimate of Mehta (1953, p. 90) shows an increase in the absolute quantity of handweaving, rather than a decline.

[34] For some specific examples of Indian quality-improvement, taken from the trade in brocades, see Harris (1993, p. 111). On low-quality Indian handwoven products, see Mehta (1953, p. 109).

specializing in high-quality products that Europeans could not imitate. Machine-made textiles could not mimic Turkish muslin, Syrian silk with gold and silver threads, or Palestinian embroidered clothes and headdresses. Available evidence indicates that weaving was on the rise throughout the nineteenth century in Egypt, Syria, and Turkey, despite European penetration into the market. The growing wealth from foreign trade increased population and the demand for cloth. The centralization of weaving in towns, which followed from the reorganization of production, boosted efficiency. As in India, European threads, twists, and yarns proved a boon to local weavers, for their lower prices and superior qualities.[35]

Some of the problems of Indian textile producers stemmed from laws, regulations, and taxes, rather than from free trade. The East India Company, which ruled parts of India until the late 1850s, promoted British economic superiority. The British textile producers of Lancashire were given free access to the Indian market, while Indian producers faced tariffs when selling to England. The British tried to make India a raw materials depot for their industries, rather than an independent competitor. In addition, Indian land was subject to prohibitive taxes, typically ranging between 50 and 75 percent, which placed Indian textile production at a competitive disadvantage.[36]

For the most part, however, English textiles succeeded in the Indian market only to the extent they met the demands of Indian consumers. Many British fabrics had superior colors and finer textures; not every Indian handicraft was a masterpiece. Many Indians found that British cloth was very comfortable, highly affordable, looked good, and fit their vision of a developing commercial society.[37]

[35] Insofar as the Egyptian textile industry experienced difficulties, it was due to the attempts of ruler Muhammad Ali to establish a government monopoly in the area. See Owen (1981, pp. 76, 93–95, 211–12, 262), and Farnie (1979, p. 104).

[36] On the land tax rates, see, for instance, Dutt (1969, p. 138), and B. Chandra (1966, p. 396). For much of the early part of the nineteenth century, the tariff duty on Indian wool coming into England was 30 percent, while British wool coming into India faced only negligible charges. This difference, however, was later eliminated, and should not be cited as a fundamental cause of market conditions. Later, in 1896 the export duty for Indian cotton was set at 3.5 percent; see Dutt (1969 [1904], pp. 114, 130, 401), and B. Chandra (1966, chap. 6).

[37] Bayley (1986, p. 308). Interestingly, English cloth made less headway in the Far East, even though it faced equivalent price advantages and arguably had a superior

To the extent that colonial Indian textiles were inferior in quality to earlier creations, a previous shrinkage of trade was partly at fault, just as in Persia. The quality of Indian handicrafts declined sharply when the Mughal empire fell in the early eighteenth century.

Between the late sixteenth and late seventeenth centuries, much of northern India enjoyed peace, prosperity, and security. Centralized Mughal rule enabled wide scope for commerce, urbanization, and cross-regional trade. During that time, the finest Mughal carpets had a silk foundation and a woolen pile made from the fleece of the mountain goat. This combination gave the textile the flexible dyeing properties of wool but the visual beauty and feel of silk. The decorations usually are based around flowering plants and latticelike designs. By most expert accounts, Indian textiles have never reattained such heights of quality.[38]

The Mughal tradition peaked in the seventeenth century and dwindled rapidly thereafter. Excellent carpets were still made during the reign of Aurangzeb (1658–1707) but the overall decline in quality was noticeable. By the time of 1739, the invasion of Nadir Shah caused the Mughal court to fall apart. Political stability ended, court demands collapsed, and trade networks shrank. Indian textiles suffered under this turn of events. As in Persia, large-scale carpetweaving remained dormant until stimulated by European demands in the nineteenth century.[39]

### The Navajos and Cross-cultural Trade

Navajo weaving also owes its existence to technology, growing wealth, and cross-cultural exchange. Handwoven Navajo textiles benefited from technological booms for over a century.

In the eighteenth century the Navajo learned weaving from other Indian tribes who had moved into the area, largely in response to the Spanish conquest. Soon the Navajo began weaving to trade with the Spanish and with other Indian tribes. The Navajo drew

---

transportation network. The English products fit better into the syncretic Indian cultural identity, thus their relative successes in that market.

[38] See J.Thompson (1988, p. 152).

[39] See Victoria and Albert Museum (1982).

their initial fabrics from the domestication of sheep and goats. Not only did the Spaniards introduce the sheep to the area, but Spanish techniques of animal husbandry allowed the Navajo to maintain much larger stocks of animals. The Navajo culture and economy therefore developed around livestock production and marketing. Herding became the most important part of the Navajo economy. These livestock were used to support an active tradition of blanket weaving and trade.[40]

Circa 1825, Navajo textiles were transformed from a purely utilitarian practice into an art. At that time the Navajo were exposed to serapes, blankets, and floor coverings from Saltillo, a region of northeastern Mexico. The serape pattern, with serrated zigzag lines, was derived from the ponchos and clothing of Spanish shepherds in Mexico, which in turn drew upon Moorish influences in Spain. Navajo design drew heavily on these sources, although the Navajos altered them to suit their own visual language, introducing deliberate distortions and eliminating the notion of border.[41]

Furthermore, industrially manufactured, dyed cloth was commonly available to the Navajo after 1821. The Navajo unraveled and rewove these materials to suit their designs. The most prized threads were the red ones, known as bayeta, unraveled from Spanish cloth, which was in turn imported by the Spanish from England (English baize). These cloths, which were not available until trade with the United States was legalized (following the 1821 Mexican Revolution), were a basis for the classic Navajo blankets. By the middle of the nineteenth century, the Navajo were using commercial Saxony woolens, often for shades of yellow and green.[42]

Imported clothes brought new colors to the Navajo. The Navajo could not produce bright reds from their vegetable dyes and there-

[40] See, for instance, Bailey and Bailey (1986, pp. 12–14) on the origin of the Navajo, and Amsden (1972).

[41] See Brody (1976). On how Africans drew from Europe for their textile designs, see Meurant (1995, pp. 113–17).

[42] See Blomberg (1988, p. 3), Deitch (1989, pp. 224–27), Kent (1976, pp. 89, 101), and Underhill (1956, p. 75). Africans also have unraveled Western machine-made textiles to make new products of high quality; see Kahlenberg (1998, p. 176).

fore depended on foreign fabrics, which they unraveled and respun for their own purposes. Ironically, the original dye for bayeta is cochineal, extracted from a beetle parasite from Mexico and reworked in Europe with advanced technologies, to be shipped back to the New World for use by American Indians. In the case of indigo dyes, also not indigenously available to the Navajo, they had been using European colorings as early as 1800.[43]

Not all the new colors had positive effects on the aesthetic quality of the product. The Navajo adopted chemical aniline dyes and aniline-dyed yarns, which had been invented in England in 1856. Aniline products quickly crossed the ocean, becoming standard in the American West with the trading post and the railroad. Three-ply yarns with the new dyes had reached the Navajo by 1865. Once these new colors were available, the Navajo experimented with them eagerly, using aniline most frequently for red. Inferior versions of the aniline dyes subsequently ran, or appeared crude and mass produced.[44]

The net effect of technology was nonetheless positive. The widespread introduction of machine-spun, raveled yarn helped improve Navajo weaving skills, just as in (East) India. The machine-made materials were finer than the native product. To effectively compete, the Navajo were forced to make their own yarns with equivalent fineness. Prespun and predyed yarns freed up Navajo labor to produce new designs, leading to such innovations as the late nineteenth century "Eyedazzlers," interlocking figures and designs with contrasting colors. Because of technology, composition increased in importance, relative to the fineness of the weave. The Eyedazzlers were considered corruptions by some critics at the time, but subsequently they have risen greatly in critical and commercial status.[45]

The later "rug period" for Navajo weaving was based on sale to distant American consumers, rather than to local trading part-

[43] See Deitch (1989, pp. 224–27), Kent (1976, pp. 89, 101), Underhill (1956, p. 75), Blomberg (1988, p. 3), and Brody (1976). On Indigo dyes, see Dedera (1975, p. 25); on cochineal, see Rodee (1981, p. 3).

[44] See Blomberg (1988, p. 5), and Haberland (1986, p. 115).

[45] On yarns, see Brody (1976). On Eyedazzlers, see Lindig (1993, pp. 111–13), and Rodee (1981, p. 5).

ners. The 1870s brought trading posts to Navajo territory, which allowed the Navajo to sell their products to settlers. The railroad reached New Mexico by the 1880s. The Navajo could now transport their wares to Americans across the country and could sell different kinds of products. The heavier rug displaced the lighter blanket by the 1890s. The change in traditional standards gave many Navajo creators the freedom to experiment and led to some of the most artistic and original of Navajo designs.[46]

Navajo styles continued to draw upon non-Navajo sources, brought by the railroad in most cases. Many late-nineteenth-century designs drew on Persian, Caucasian, and Turkish textiles, largely because trading-post operators encouraged the Navajo to incorporate them into their work. The Navajo arts incorporated far more than Spanish and American influences, showing again how wealth and technology can spur human creativity.[47]

---

[46] See Lindig (1993, pp. 111–13), and Kahlenberg and Berlant (1972, p. 25).

[47] On Oriental influences, see Haberland (1986, p. 119), and Kaufman and Selser (1985, p. 72).

# 3
### ■ Ethos and the Tragedy of Cultural Loss

The power of wealth and technology has helped common commercial influences spread to unprecedented degree. At last count, the games of the National Basketball Association can be seen in over 100 countries, Toyotas can be bought in 151 countries, and Coca-Cola can be purchased in 185 countries. Each year McDonald's opens twice as many restaurants abroad as in the United States. The automobile, the suburban development, and the shopping mall attract new customers around the globe.[1]

The practical benefits of these developments are obvious, and they have been accompanied by explosions of cultural creativity, as discussed in the last chapter. Yet despite this significant upside we cannot help but feel that something cultural is lost at the same time. To explicate what that loss might be, I consider when cross-cultural contact damages ethos in poorer and smaller societies. *Destruction of ethos* can cause non-Western cultures to lose their uniqueness, thereby faltering in their artistic creativity.

While this book is about what kinds of freedom are possible in the modern world, we cannot understand freedom without tragedy.

[1] See Orvell (1995, p. 147), Shenk (1997, p. 110), and Waters (1995, p. 70).

It turns out that the greater the scope of cultural booms around the world, the greater the degree of cultural tragedy as well.

As we will see further below, the concept of ethos helps us see the link between cultural creativity and cultural corruption. By *ethos* I mean the special feel or flavor of a culture. Ethos can be considered the background network of worldviews, styles, and inspirations found in a society, or a framework for cultural interpretation. Ethos therefore is part of an implicit language for creating or viewing art. More specifically, ethos may consist of societal self-confidence, the worldview generated by collective adherence to a religion, or cultural presuppositions about the nature and importance of beauty. Ethos often involves tacit or background knowledge that informs what we do but resists written or verbal formulation. French historian and philosopher of art Hippolyte Taine referred to "the general state of mind and surrounding circumstances." The German words *Weltanschauung* (way of looking at the world) and *Zeitgeist* (spirit of the times) express the notion more precisely than any English language equivalent.[2]

The combination of ethos and technique gives a creative era its particular "feel," or its stylistic and emotional core. Historical environment helped breed strength and confidence in the music of Beethoven and Chopin, grit and messianic fervor in Jamaican reggae, and nobility and grandeur in the paintings of the Florentine Renaissance. The educated viewer or listener has little trouble recognizing a Renaissance painting as Florentine, or a piece of music as Jamaican, even though diverse particular styles proliferated in each locale and their derivations have spread elsewhere.

Creators experience similar influences in their formative years, which supports commonality of style. They have had the same teachers, seen the same images, and grown up in the same environment. The desire to appeal to a given audience transmits commonal-

---

[2] See Taine (1980 [1865], p. 95). Mannheim (1952) provides one account of ethos, emphasizing the German notion of Weltanschauung. On ethos in scientific communities, see Crane (1972). For background on the theory of Taine, see Munro (n.d., especially chap. 8).

ity as well. Creators often seek fame, the approval of their customers and peers, or they enjoy being able to stir an audience. These motives spur artists to communicate an aesthetic sensibility that is "in tune" with their customers, and thus consonant with the spirit of their time. Artistic products then further shape that spirit and extend its influence, giving rise to a two-way process of cumulative feedback.

An ethos does not require unanimity of opinion. British youth culture of the 1960s consisted of the clash between "Mods" and "Rockers." These two groups *dis*agreed about a common set of questions in a common framework, and in that sense they shared an ethos. It has been remarked that "opposites are exactly alike, save for one difference." Ethos is a shared cultural matrix for interpretation, rather than a narrow conformity of opinion.

In economic language, ethos refers to the interdependence of individual attitudes, or to a "network effect" across attitudes, to use the more technical phrase. The attitude held by one person is, in part, a function of the attitudes held by others in the same community. In terms of a formal economic model, ethos is an unpriced, untraded input into production, collectively produced by the actions and attitudes of many human beings.

Ethos, by its nature, cannot be defined with complete rigor. Its intangible nature resists definitive characterization, much like the concept of "paradigm" in the philosophy of science. Nonetheless it would be unfair to the critics of cross-cultural trade to dismiss the concept on such grounds. Cross-cultural contacts change how people think about the world, and such changes in thinking have broader ramifications for artistic production, not always for the better.

A favorable ethos can help relatively small groups achieve cultural miracles. Classical Periclean Athens had fewer than two-hundred thousand residents (and even fewer free citizens), according to best estimates, but its creative accomplishments in philosophy, poetry, history, drama, and politics remain nonpareil. The Athenians were not genetically superior to the moderns, but their age offered a favorable moral temperament for bold and creative thinking. Athens imbued its creators with a burning sense of discovery and wonder, a sense of doing things for the first time.[3]

The population of Renaissance Florence did not typically exceed eighty thousand and at times fell well below that figure. To put the Florentine achievement in proper perspective with regard to population, consider that in 1984 approximately thirty-five thousand painters, sculptors, potters, and art historians graduated from American art schools. I have stressed the favorable economic conditions behind Florentine art elsewhere, but, no less importantly, the Florentine environment emphasized the wonders of art in complementary civic, humanistic, and religious dimensions.[4] The Florentines also identified with their city as a creative center, rather than as a military power or as part of an empire. An ethos of strength, optimism, and humanism shines through in Florentine works to this day. Most significantly, the Florentines saw art as *important*, an attitude that drove such a small population to produce so much creative output.[5]

The importance of ethos is universal to culture, and is not restricted to the West. Haitian voodoo art, Hong Kong action cinema, and Cuban dance music, among many other artistic examples, all draw a special feel from their home cultures. Their creators regard their respective enterprises as important, and worthy of their deepest creative efforts. As in Athens or Florence, ethos helps relatively small numbers of people achieve miraculous creative blossomings.

## ■ Fragility and the Problems of Ethos

Ethos makes globalization a nontrivial problem for culture. There is little danger that economic growth, international trade, and the spread of technical knowledge will bring inferior-quality hammers, refrigerators, or vacuum cleaners either to the United States or to lesser developed nations. In each of these sectors or industries,

---

[3] On the population of Athens, see Sinclair (1988, p. 9).
[4] See Cowen (1998).
[5] On the art school figure, see Robert Hughes (1991, p. 401).

knowledge dissemination has unambiguously positive effects and creates more and better opportunities for all parties involved.

Trade and economic growth, however, do not guarantee the progress of culture in the same direct manner. Unlike in ordinary commercial sectors, more knowledge does not necessarily result in culture that earns higher critical acclaim. An ethos, which by definition is a unique perspective on the world, can be weakened or destroyed by external commercial influences, even if those influences improve human welfare in the broader sense. The clustering of cultural knowledge in time and space, as discussed above and throughout this book, reflects the scarcity, uniqueness, and fragility of ethos.

Ironically, artists can lose their creativity in certain genres if they learn too much about other approaches. Contemporary musician Beck, an eclectic purveyor of rock, country, and blues made the point succinctly: "You can't write a pure country song any more. You can't write a pure Appalachian ballad. Because we live in a world where we've all heard speed-metal, we've all heard drum-and-bass, we've all heard old-school hip-hop. Even if you're not influenced by it, or you're not using elements of it, they're in your mind."[6]

Before the widespread advent of recording and radio, different parts of Europe had their own schools of classical conducting, violin playing, and pianism, each with a recognizable sound. Electronic reproduction, by spreading knowledge of these styles, has limited their number. To an increasing degree, classical musicians sound alike, albeit at a very high level of technical excellence. The communication and exchange of ideas has brought the initially disparate musical visions closer together. In similar fashion, many "Naive" painters from underdeveloped locales lose the uniqueness of their style, once they are exposed to Western artworks.

No modern Western writer holds or could hold the worldview behind Dante's *Divine Comedy.* For better or worse, the moral force of hell has been lost amongst the intelligentsia. The contemporary

---

[6] Pareles (1998, p. 40).

New York intellectual cannot think of hell without modern irony and satire bubbling to the surface, or perhaps even ridicule. Many episodes of the television show *Seinfeld* confirm the change in perspective.

Hegel was overreacting when he described irony as the death of art, as he had little sense of the possibilities of the postmodern. Nonetheless he understood how irony could sap the heroic temperament of art or limit its aesthetic aspirations. Andy Warhol's "Last Supper" paintings are masterpieces in their own right, but most modern American artists cannot portray "the grandeur of Christ" in the same manner that medieval or Renaissance painters could. Proust's *Remembrance of Things Past* would not have been the same book had he not taken the aristocracy seriously at some level, however much he ridiculed it.

Unlike many forms of technical knowledge, artistic capabilities cannot be transferred easily to other eras or to other societies. The Navajo, despite their formidable weaving talents, cannot produce a first-rate Amish quilt. Not only do they lack the refined technical knowledge for Amish production, but they do not possess the proper feel for the aesthetic, any more than the Amish could produce a first-rate Navajo blanket. Today's Navajo cannot replicate the feel and quality of their most famous products from the 1860s, although large profits would await them if they could.

No matter how much money were spent, it would be difficult to make a Persian carpet as spectacular as the best Safavid works from the sixteenth or seventeenth centuries. In part the relevant network of knowledge, training, and expertise no longer exists. But in part modern day Iran no longer has the same cultural self-confidence and does not hold the same relative place in the world order. Although handwoven carpets remain common and command an extraordinary quantity of resources, they do not match the best of the earlier works in quality or current market price. The greater riches and technology of modern-day Iran do not make up for these deficiencies.

It is a moot point whether the new cultural possibilities are better than the older, now-impossible styles. The point is that in the production of culture, more knowledge does not expand our opportunities across all fronts. Rather, growth brings a trade-off between one set of styles and another.

Too much knowledge, or knowledge of the wrong kind, can limit creativity. In this regard (among others), the economics of culture offers unique problems. Retrogression in production is not only possible, it is common and significant.

We see a parallel with contemporary macroeconomic theory here. Modern "real" business-cycle theory relies on the idea of a negative productivity shock—a decrease in the efficiency of producing goods and services—to bring an economic downturn. Commentators have suggested that negative productivity shocks are inappropriate for modern economies, since we do not forget how to produce most items. In fact the idea is one of the most profound contributions of modern business-cycle theory, and it has special relevance to the world of art and culture. The way we make many products—most of all culture—depends critically on our background assumptions, which are subject to change for the worse. Ironically, in the case of culture, the "negative technology shock" often consists of *acquiring* knowledge, not losing it.

Some degree of *isolation* can inject self-confidence and a sense of magic into an art. Many Third World and indigenous artisans view their crafts as imbued with great religious and mythic significance, and as having central importance for the unfolding of history. In reality, they may be "just another craftsperson" in the eyes of the outside world, but their creativity will be greater if this knowledge is not rubbed in their faces. Furthermore, exotic goods and technologies from richer societies can take away status from native creations. In this regard, the "power relations" described by Marxists can limit the creativity of smaller or poorer societies.

Ethos often is based on a sense of missionary zeal that is not strictly justified by the objective facts. Art and creative power, to some extent, rest on illusion and delusion, most of all in the minds of artists. If the voodoo religion of Haiti were definitively revealed to be untrue to all Haitians, Haitian art would be much poorer for it. It is commonly said that the country of Haiti is 90 percent Catholic and 100 percent voodoo (*vodou*). Selden Rodman, the American patron saint of Haitian art, described the Haitians as "insulated against the ravages of visual propaganda, photography, and scepticism." In other words, false consciousness is a wellspring of human creativity.[7]

The problems of ethos-disruption are of two kinds. First, the disappearance of the earlier culture, and its accompanying artistic products, may be undesirable for some intrinsic ethical or aesthetic reason. Second, we can think of the problem in terms of the preferences of the community members. Too much trade, or trade of the wrong kind, could make the trading individuals worse off, due to the collective secondary consequences of those trades for the cultural in the long run.

The logic here is straightforward. Individuals in a smaller, poorer culture typically benefit from adopting the innovations from the larger, richer culture. They live longer, receive more consumer goods, and enjoy discovering the new cultures they encounter. Yet individuals in the smaller culture do not prefer each and every aspect of their new fate. From the point of view of these individuals, the two cultures have more contact with each other than would be ideal. The smaller culture would prefer to receive the benefits of trade but keep out the ethos of the larger culture to a greater degree. Each individual in the smaller culture, when trading with the larger culture, does not internalize the costs of ethos-disruption that result. For this reason, the smaller culture, as a whole, may end up trading with the larger culture more than the individuals in the smaller culture prefer. Creative artists, of course, cannot hold themselves aloof from far-reaching processes of these kinds, and their worldviews will change as well.

[7] Rodman (1961, p. 105).

The larger culture might benefit from less trade as well, or bene-fit from trade of different kinds. Members of the larger culture would prefer to keep receiving the unique products of the smaller culture. North Americans would be worse off if the Inuit lost their ability to produce their unique sculptures, carvings, and prints. If non-Inuit people have too much contact with Inuit culture, or con-tacts of the wrong kinds, they will make it harder for the Inuit to produce high-quality works. This kind of artistic spoiling, however, arises through a cumulative effect, so most individuals do not take such worries into account when deciding how much contact to have with the Inuit.

The causes of ethos-disruption are often consumer-driven, and in that sense they advance progress and human welfare. Many Kingston workers *want* to eat at McDonald's, even if it costs them a day's pay. But if too many Jamaicans do the same on a regular basis, Jamaican society may become less unique. The resulting transforma-tion may alter or destroy the Jamaican potential for distinctive cre-ative visions. Reggae music could not have flourished without the recording studio, a product of advanced technology, but at the same time reggae would lose its special feel, and thus its contribution to global variety, if Kingston became too much like Beverly Hills.

## ■ The Minerva Model

Cross-cultural contact often mobilizes the creative fruits of an ethos before disrupting or destroying it. In this regard trade plays a criti-cal and neglected role in converting an ethos into creative artistic achievement.

We see a common pattern. The initial meeting of cultures pro-duces a creative boom, as individuals trade materials, technologies, and ideas. Often the materially wealthier culture provides financial support for the creations of the poorer culture, while the native aes-thetic and ethos remains largely intact. For a while we have the best of both worlds from a cultural point of view. The core of the poorer or smaller culture remains intact, while it benefits from trade. Over time, however, the larger or wealthier culture upsets the balance of forces that ruled in the smaller or poorer culture. The poorer culture begins to direct its outputs towards the tastes of the richer culture. Communication with the outside world makes the prevailing ethos less distinct. The smaller culture "forgets" how to make the high-quality goods it once specialized in, and we observe cultural decline.

I refer to this as the *Minerva model*. In this scenario a burst of creative flowering also brings the decline of a culture and an ethos. Even when two (or more) cultures do not prove compatible in the long run, they may produce remarkable short-run gains from trade. "Minerva" refers to Hegel's famous statement that "the owl of Minerva flies only at dusk," by which he meant that philosophic understanding of a civilization comes only when that civilization has already realized its potential and is in decline. I reinterpret the metaphor to refer to cultural brilliance instead, which in this context occurs just when a particular culture is starting its decline. Alternatively, it may be said that cultural blossomings contain the seeds of their own destruction.

The culture of the Hawaiian Islands, rather than withering immediately with foreign contact, blossomed in the late nineteenth and early twentieth centuries. The combination of Pacific, American, Japanese, and Chinese influences created a fertile creative environment. In music Hawaiian performers have been seminal influences behind the development of country and western, pedal steel guitar, blues, jazz, and fingerpicking guitar styles, as well as modern "lounge" music. In each case the Hawaiians innovated within established Western forms, or relied partly on Western inspiration. The Hawaiian steel guitar, for instance, was invented by a Czech immigrant living in California. Hawaii also produced many superb hand-woven quilts in the latter part of the nineteenth century and in the early part of the twentieth. Like Hawaiian music, these works were synthetic products of American, Asian, and Polynesian styles.[8]

---

[8] On Hawaiian quilts, see Wild (1987). On the guitar, see Clifford (1997, p. 26).

This fertile period for Hawaiian culture, however, did not last forever. American dominance of the island—in cultural, economic, and political terms—was only a matter of time. The vital indigenous Hawaiian culture has since dwindled precipitously, having been swamped by the greater numbers and wealth of mainland Americans and Asians. Contemporary Hawaii is hardly a cultural desert (witness the architecture at Diamond Head), but it is more like mainland America than in times past. The region is not producing a stream of distinctive creative achievement comparable to its peak years earlier in this century.

To damn modernity for this development, however, ignores the original role of cross-cultural contact in stimulating the creative environment. Virtually all of the Hawaiian innovations were synthetic in nature and based in cultural trade. In part, modernity destroys so many cultural communities only by creating so many in the first place. And the original sources behind Hawaiian culture—such as the Chinese, Japanese, and Polynesian components—were themselves synthetic products of earlier eras. They arose from earlier processes of creative destruction, which had left many cultural victims in their wake as well.

The Minerva model applies most frequently when gains from trade are based on a severe cultural imbalance. For instance, American Indian arts and crafts flourished until shortly before their (temporary) collapse early in the twentieth century. The most accomplished arts of the Plains Indians used European crayons, pencils, clothes, metals, bright paint-pigments, papers, dyed-wool yarns, mirrors, bells, brass tacks, and glass beads. The wood-splint basketry technique of many Indian tribes appears to have been European in origin, probably Swedish. The kachina dolls of the Hopi flowered in the nineteenth century, when the Hopi tribe came into contact with Spanish and Mexican folk art, and sought to meet touristic demands for dolls.[9]

---

[9] On Hopi kachina, see Furst and Furst (1982, p. 31). Some scholars note the possibility that the kachina may have preceded Spanish contact, but even they admit a strong influence; see, for instance, Dockstader (1954, p. 98). On the Plains Indians

Indian totem poles became common in the middle of the nineteenth century when the Northwest fur trade brought new wealth to Indian communities. Indian chiefs and nobles competed for status by commissioning large poles; a major village would have as many as seventy. Large numbers of impressive poles became feasible only after settlers introduced the metal knife, a prerequisite for effective large-scale Indian carving. Across North America, trade relations gave an unprecedented boost to Indian artistic production in the eighteenth and nineteenth centuries. This was exactly when the North American Indian cultures, viewed more broadly as a way of life, were declining precipitously.[10]

The tradition of Andean textiles was badly damaged by Spanish conquest, but Andean weaving boomed during the early years of contact with Europeans. On the demand side, some of the Spaniards recognized that Andean textiles were of very high quality and bought them eagerly, thus stimulating production. On the supply side, the Andean weavers drew upon new materials, styles, and ideas. The Spaniards introduced silk, linen, sheep's wool, and metal-wrapped threads, in addition to bringing stylistic inspiration in the forms of textiles and designs from Europe, the Arab world, Turkey, and China. In particular, the Andean weavers innovated with their use of color, which they started using in complex patterns to create effects of depth and dimensionality. Chinese silk tapestries and embroideries, brought in through the Philippines, were especially influential. Until the Spanish toll on the Andean societies became decisively high and destroyed their social infrastructure, the cross-cultural contact proved fruitful for the textile arts.[11]

---

arts, see Feder (1986, p. 93, passim), and Brody (1971, p. 25); on basketry techniques, see J.G.H. King (1986, p. 82), and Sturtevant (1986, p. 33). For other examples of Indian synthesis, see Feest (1992, pp. 42–44, 107). Egan (1993, chap. 6) and Damian (1995, pp. 44–45) discusses the role of Indian painters and craftsmen in colonial art in South America.

[10] See Woodcock (1977, p. 25), and H. Stewart (1990, pp. 20–21). On the roles of knives, see Feder (1971, p.18). The totem pole tradition was discontinued in the later-nineteenth century when the fur trade slowed down, smallpox eradicated many villages, the rifle led to bloody intertribal warfare, and the Canadian government outlawed many elements of Indian culture.

[11] See Stone-Miller (1992, pp. 51–60, 185–86, 193–96, 201).

The Minerva model implies that it may be worthwhile to "cash in" the potential creativity embedded in a culture. By accepting the eventual decline of the culture, we also are mobilizing its creative forces to unprecedented levels, at least for a while.

The modern world may be cashing in cultures too quickly, or too many at once, but we should not measure failure by the number of declining cultures. Casual observers too quickly conclude that an observed decline suggests a problem. But the absence of observed cultural decline could be a sign of failure rather than success. The absence of decline might reflect a world that attained less diversity in the first place and reached lower and fewer peaks. Conversely, a large number of declining artistic genres might be a symptom of cultural wealth and vitality, rather than a harbinger of complete and absolute decay for all time.

Most generally, almost all of today's disappearing cultures evolved out of earlier processes of remixing and "cashing in" of cultures. The spread of the Chinese across Southeast Asia, the extension of the Roman Empire, or the European folk migrations in the Dark Ages, whatever their cultural benefits, all wrought great havoc on the cultures of their time. In reality today's so-called indigenous cultures are regroupings, yesterday's remixed version of previous cultural expansions. Cross-cultural contact cashes in some cultures while others germinate. Subsequent exchanges will bring out the virtues of these cultures-in-waiting, while simultaneously heralding their later declines.

## ■ Trade and Ethos

We should not cast trade as the villain in this process of ongoing cultural reshuffling, even though trade sometimes destroys ethos. Paradoxically, the successful development of an ethos relies on trade as well as on isolation. It is no accident that Classical civilization developed in the Mediterranean, where cultures used sea transport to trade with each other and learn from each other. Trade relations spread the spirit of learning throughout Europe during late medieval times, starting in northern France, the Low Countries, and Italy. The mobility of scholars, painters, manuscripts, and scientific ideas gave birth to the Renaissance. The development of the United States, another formative event in Western history, owes its existence to trade and resource mobility. Virtually every ethos owes its existence to cross-cultural contact in some form or another.

Cross-cultural contact continues to support ethos growth today. The popular music of the Cape Verde Islands has a recognizable feel, even though the population on the islands is less than four hundred thousand. Partial isolation has allowed a unique style to incubate. At the same time, Cape Verdean music, and the Cape Verdean way of life, is explicitly synthetic in nature, mixing Portuguese, African, Brazilian, and other influences. If not for maritime trade, including the lucrative slave trade, the islands would not have been settled. Remittances from Cape Verdeans working abroad subsidize life at home and the musical community.

The Jamaican musical ethos did not take off until African-American rhythm and blues were imported. Jamaican migrant sugar workers were exposed to rhythm and blues during their trips to the American South in the late 1940s, and they brought back a taste for the music. Later, Jamaican listeners picked up rhythm-and-blues broadcasts from New Orleans and Miami radio during the 1950s. Louis Jordan, Fats Domino, Shirley and Lee, Bill Doggett, Roscoe Gordon, Ernie Freeman, and Chuck Berry were especially popular in Jamaica. (Jamaicans tended to prefer loping, less hurried rhythms, rather than the Delta blues of Howlin' Wolf and Muddy Waters, and this continues to be reflected in reggae music.) The Jamaican ska tunes of the early 1960s, the first breakthrough for Jamaican music, reveal strong influences from doo-wop, swing, crooners, and the softer forms of rhythm and blues. Sam Cooke and Nat King Cole remain beloved in Jamaica to this day.[12]

Even apparent instances of extreme isolation often rely heavily on trade. The Ayala brothers (Juan Camilo, Marcial Camilo, and Felix Camilo), three Mexican folk painters, live in the mountain vil-

---

[12] See Chang and Chen (1998, pp. 19–25).

lage of San Agustin Oapan in the state of Guerrero. The ascent to this village requires several hours' drive on the highway (from either Mexico City or Acapulco) and then a lengthy drive on a largely dirt road. Only in the lifetime of the brothers has the village had electricity. The Ayalas learnt Spanish only later in their lives, as their native tongue is the pre-Hispanic Nahuatl. The village has no more than a few thousand inhabitants (the number varies seasonally) and supports unique styles of drawing and painting, shared only by several neighboring villages. We thus see that this creative environment is marked by considerable isolation.[13]

The role of trade in this story is less obvious but no less important. Village artisans first started painting on bark paper in the early 1960s. Max Kerlow, an architect and movie actor from Mexico City, also ran a crafts shop, which sold largely to tourists. When some of the village artisans visited him, he suggested that bark paper (*amate*) drawings could be more easily marketed and transported than pottery, with its high rates of breakage. Until that time, the village painters had not thought of working with bark paper, which comes from another part of Mexico (San Pablito, in the state of Puebla). In these early days American Mary Price, sister of the movie actor Vincent Price, was an important patroness of the art.

The Ayalas were the first village artisans to paint on board and canvas. Marcial Camilo Ayala, purely by accident, was befriended by an American, Ed Rabkin, when Marcial left the village to sell his wares in the streets of Cuernavaca. Rabkin gave Marcial and his brothers the appropriate artistic materials, supported them for several years, and marketed their works to North American collectors. Since that time the paintings of the Ayalas have been funded primarily by foreign demand. More generally, the village, San Agustin Oapan, has found economic sustenance, and thus has preserved much of its way of life, by selling pottery and bark paintings to outsiders, often tourists. The village inhabitants have resisted absorption into larger urban areas by cultivating the arts and crafts. Em-

---

[13] I have benefited from conversations with the relevant parties, including the Ayalas and Max Kerlow. See also Amith (1995). I am planning a subsequent work, a case study of globalization, devoted solely to the Ayalas and San Agustin Oapan.

beddedness in a larger culture has given the Ayalas, and the other artisans from their area, a favorable mix of isolation and cross-cultural contact.

## ■ The Importance of Size and Critical Mass

When trying to sustain an independent ethos, cultures face a problem of critical mass. No single individual, acting on his or her own, can produce an ethos. Rather, an ethos results from the interdependent acts of many individuals. This cluster of produced meaning may require some degree of insulation from larger and wealthier outside forces.

The Canadian Inuit maintain their own ethos, even though they number no more than twenty-four thousand. They manage this feat through a combination of trade, to support their way of life, and geographic isolation. The Inuit occupy remote territory, removed from major population centers of Canada. If cross-cultural contact were to become sufficiently close, the Inuit ethos would disappear. Distinct cultural groups of similar size do not, in the long run, persist in downtown Toronto, where they come in contact with many outside influences and pursue essentially Western paths for their lives.

Critical mass matters. Before the twentieth century, few people traveled and travel occurred in large groups only rarely. The charge was that tourism would corrupt the traveler, and that he would lose his national and cultural allegiance. The English regarded travel as leading to "Italienate" vices, for instance. Today tourism is practiced en masse. Given this fact, contemporary critics charge that travelers corrupt the places they visit, a possibility that had not occurred to earlier critics. The English now are accused of ruining Italy, rather than being ruined by Italy. The problem is most extreme in small, island nations. In 1990 the Bahamas received fourteen tourists for each native, and St. Maarten received twenty-four for each native.[14]

[14] On earlier critiques of travel, see Warneke (1995). On the Caribbean, see Krotz (1996, p. 11).

The more populous and economically large the culture, the less risk it runs of being swamped by cross-cultural contact. It will be able to absorb foreign ideas without being overwhelmed by them. Japan, the United States, and Germany are three examples of cultures that absorb numerous outside influences, and evolve accordingly, but without losing their identity.

The larger society usually possesses a greater resiliency to external shocks and offers greater opportunities for regrouping. The diversity within a large society increases the chance that some of its parts will respond flexibly and creatively to foreign influence, even if other parts are corrupted. In this regard the larger society is more diversified and better protected against outside risk.

Foreign penetration and influence will take more time to reach all the nooks and crannies of the larger society. Native customs therefore persist for longer periods of time in their original forms, which increases the chance of a fruitful synthesis between the two cultures. The large, insulated native culture can draw upon the foreign innovations at its own pace, adopting or rejecting them as is seen fit. In contrast, when foreign influences hit all of a smaller society at once, fruitful adaptation may be more difficult to achieve.

The larger society is also more likely to be synthetic in the first place, and thus better adapted to absorbing and transforming foreign influences. Brazil, America, and Canada are essentially nations of voluntary or forced immigrants, and therefore have developed infrastructures to mediate foreign elements. These institutions may include greater public acceptance of inequality and difference, a relatively universal popular culture, political tolerance, and national "myths" that favor or enable change, such as the American notion of the "melting pot" or the more recent Canadian concept of coexisting cultures.

In the less-developed world, Mexico and India provide models of how large societies can maintain distinct and diverse identities in conjunction with extensive foreign contact. Mexico, for instance, consists of numerous culturally independent regions with dozens of mutually unintelligible languages. The country offers a remarkable variety of cuisines and arts and crafts. This diversity has proven highly resilient to foreign influences, as Mexico has been culturally synthetic from at least the beginning of its historic records. Modern Mexican regional diversity owes much of its existence to the railroad and to the economic growth of Mexico, which funded a cultural boom, starting in the early part of the twentieth century.

Mexican creativity continues to flourish, in a wide variety of forms, ranging from contemporary art to cinema to Mexican rap music. Even in the folk arts, the number of artisans in Mexico is now at an all-time high.[15]

East Indian culture exhibits a recurring historical pattern of being swamped by some outside culture, digesting that culture after a period of adjustment, and returning with synthetic innovations of a very high quality. The Aryan invaders brought Sanskrit and the gods of the Vedas. The Hellenic influence came to India at the time of Alexander, heavily influencing Gandharan sculpture. Later, India had extensive seaborne trade with the Roman Empire. The Islamic influence transformed Indian arts and architecture from the thirteenth century onwards. The Persian influence was especially important in the earlier years of the Mughal Empire, stretching from the sixteenth century to the rule of Queen Victoria (1526–1857). The first two-hundred years of this period often are considered the peak of Indian culture. The Taj Mahal at Agra comes from Persian sources and influence. The Persian influence was dominant in the decorative arts as well, but again India responded by absorbing and transforming foreign ideas. The British and Western influence in India has been no exception to this pattern. India is now a world leader in cinema, the novel, and popular music, all genres that owe a considerable debt to Western contact.[16]

It is well known that Polynesian self-confidence and creativity were damaged by European colonialism and trade. This should not

[15] See Canclíni (1993).

[16] For a history of foreign influence in India, see Singhal (1969). On the Hellenic influence on Indian sculpture, see P. Chandra (1981, p. 37). On the Roman connection, see Warmington (1974).

come as a total surprise, given the numbers involved: at the time of contact, it is estimated that the population of Tahiti was no more than thirty-five thousand.[17]

It is less commonly recognized that the Europeans did much of their damage by *cutting off* cross-cultural contact amongst the Polynesians themselves. The critical mass behind precolonial Polynesian culture operated across great distances of time and space and was formed over centuries of cross-cultural trade. Advanced seafaring technologies allowed the Polynesians to develop cultures more sophisticated than the population of any single island could support. The processes of cultural diffusion and synthesis across islands, however, were relatively slow and limited, at least compared to the impact of nineteenth-century European technologies. When the Europeans arrived, each island faced the Western presence alone and without a secure footing in a larger population and culture. The European interveners rapidly became the locus of cross-cultural contact, thereby making the culture of each island more isolated and more vulnerable. The Polynesian islands no longer could evolve together as a single, connected macro-culture. Each island became "culturally smaller" at the same time that it encountered the traumatic shock of contact with the Europeans.[18]

For these reasons, globalization tends to encourage large, internally diverse polities, rather than small, unique ones. When the small, previously unique societies come in contact with the rest of the world they tend to lose their uniqueness. Nonetheless the smaller societies feed into the broader cultural stream, in Hegelian fashion. The cultural entities that survive tend to be large but to have complex and diverse inner workings.

The evolution of languages reflects similar trends in the evolution of diversity. There is no doubt that modernization reduces the number of global languages, and in that regard limits diversity; at least half of the world's six thousand languages are likely to die out in the next century.

[17] See Withey (1987, p. 266).
[18] On this point, see *A New Oceania* (1993).

We should not conclude, however, that linguistic diversity is decreasing in all regards. Each surviving language offers greater richness than before. English has more words than ever before, and a greater body of written material, including more translated works from other languages. Fiction has more writers and more genres, popular and technical science books are multiplying, and local versions of English are continuing to evolve in India, the Caribbean, and many other places. We cannot give any simple answer as to whether linguistic diversity is rising or falling. The number of great differences between languages is becoming smaller, but, as with culture, each language contains more diversity within.

The printing press, a vehicle for literary globalization, brought similarly complex effects on diversity. In the early days of the printing press, it was widely believed that it would ensure the dominance of Latin at the expense of local European dialects. This prediction was not confirmed. Instead, the printing press helped establish numerous national languages as viable intellectual and literary competitors to Latin. Each of these languages developed into a far richer and more diverse medium of expression, and in that regard diversity rose. At the same time, within each region a single language, usually a local dialect in origin, was elevated to national status at the expense of linguistic competitors. The number and influence of dialects declined, and in that regard diversity fell.[19]

## ▧ Ethos, Broad and Narrow

The Minerva scenario does not unambiguously destroy ethos but, rather, changes the nature of ethos. As we might expect from cross-cultural contact, it supports a greater diversity of ethos within each

---

[19] For the prediction about the printing press, see Newcomb (1996, p. 107). The logic of evolutionary biology illustrates other trade-offs between conflicting notions of diversity. Isolated pockets of a population can evolve more rapidly into new and different species precisely because they do not breed regularly with the larger population. If a radical and beneficial mutation develops in the smaller population, it may be more likely to persist, given that it will not be watered down by contact with the larger population. On the other hand, the larger pocket of population develops more small variations. It has more initial diversity to work with, and a larger genetic pool for experimentation. I am indebted to Robin Hanson for this observation.

society, while limiting diversity across societies. Previous ethoses move closer together, and therefore cease to make artistic production distinct in varying locales. They are replaced, however, by a greater number of partial or niche ethoses. These new ethoses are less general and all-embracing than those from the past.

Ethoses vary in their comprehensiveness and their totality. Some ethoses, such as those embedded in many tribal religions, embrace and cover virtually all aspects of life, including family life, sex, art, and village social structure. Other ethoses are far more limited and cover only a few areas of life. The "programmer culture" of Silicon Valley, football fandom, or teenage "rave culture" of the late 1980s and 1990s are a few examples of ethos in the narrower and more modest sense. These ethoses provide ways of thinking about particular problems, art forms, or endeavors, but they do not have a comprehensive general reach. I will refer to *broad ethos* and *narrow ethos*, to cover the two cases.

The same processes that limit the number of broad ethoses in the world also stimulate the development of new narrow ethoses in each society. Economic development and cross-cultural exchange make the ethoses in a society more diverse, more diffuse, and less all-embracing.

We observe exactly this kind of evolution in American cultural history. The spread of newspapers, books, and magazines did much to weaken American cultural regionalism. The information and ideas available in Arkansas, for example, no longer differed so drastically from what was available in New Hampshire. This was a homogenizing tendency. At the same time, the communication of information across space allowed for the mobilization of new constituencies—not geographically centered—with unique outlooks in niche areas of culture.

To provide an example, the science fiction revolution of the mid-twentieth century would not have been possible without national networks for publishing and distribution. Few science fiction books and periodicals could have supported themselves by selling to purely local audiences. Although science fiction is a small part of life for most people, it is nonetheless associated with a kind of ethos.

The spread of science fiction helped shape a core of readers and writers with common presuppositions and concerns. Science fiction readers hardly agree on all matters, but they are more likely to ponder the importance of space travel, robots, and contact with nonhuman cultures. This broad set of common concerns has spawned creative achievement in literature, cinema, and computer games; for instance, many of the films of Steven Spielberg and George Lucas are unimaginable without this background. The ethos of late twentieth century American science fiction is unmistakable, yet science fiction fans and writers have never had a well-defined geographic or regional core.

Nor do science fiction fans share an entire and unique worldview in the same way that members of a tribe in Papua New Guinea might. The science fiction ethos applies to one or a few spheres of life, rather than providing a comprehensive approach to all reality. There is no "science fiction" way of cooking or painting, for instance. Most science fiction fans and writers hold mainstream perspectives about such matters. The same can be said about most modern niche ethoses, including hippie culture, cyberpunk, "computer geek" culture, "cosmo girl" culture, and yuppie culture, among many others.

The resulting small, partial cultural communities are typically independent of geography, as their ethoses are transmitted through means other than spatial proximity. We can speak of the liberation of ethos from geography, rather than the destruction of ethos.

The Internet, the most recent revolution in cultural broadcasting, is well suited for the mobilization and discovery of narrow ethoses of these kinds. It brings together fans who live in different parts of the world, and supports and creates narrow ethoses by coordinating in this fashion.

The more that national or international communications replace geographic and regionally defined culture, the greater the impetus for the proliferation of narrow ethoses. Homogenization implies a pool of customers who receive common information from common outside sources, whether it be newspapers, television, or the Internet. Once these individuals have been brought into a common pool with well-developed means of communication, however, they sort themselves into more finely grained and more diverse groups. Entrepreneurs will create new groups by marketing, and new groups evolve by mobility and sorting. This finer sorting into more narrow ethoses need not break down the initial homogenizing trend but, rather, can coexist with it. The same individual can be a fan of Madonna and television soap operas while contributing to the ethos behind rave music and cyberpunk. In these cases heterogenization and homogenization are complementary developments rather than opposing processes. Many kinds of internal diversification occur only when a society becomes larger and in some regards more homogeneous. Counterintuitively, modern diversity *relies on* homogenizing trends to some degree.

The contemporary phenomenon of "ethnic revival" does not militate against these trends, but in fact fits the modern phenomenon of the multiplication of many kinds of narrow ethos. Today many smaller cultures appear to be undergoing a resurgence. The popular press has devoted great attention to the phenomenon of ethnic revival in recent times. Some dying languages, such as Welsh, Basque, and Yiddish, are attracting new interest. American Indian communities are devoting more time and effort to preserving their heritage, to cite another example. Ethnically based secession movements have gained in strength in many quarters.

These phenomena are often misunderstood. The developments are new ethoses of a narrow kind, rather than a return towards older, geographically distinct ethoses of the broad and all-embracing kind. Western and universalistic perspectives continue to permeate these groups and exert strong influences. In reality, the revival of ethnic identity is coming in a few select and carefully carved-out spheres of life. Most of these groups no longer hold a distinct ethos as an all-embracing totality. It is common, for instance, for these groups to organize using the Internet and cell phones, rather than to call a community meeting by word of mouth.

The new, narrow kinds of ethos do correspond to older distinct and broad ethoses from the past, and in this regard it may appear that the older ethos is being revived. More accurately, the older traditions are being reincarnated in terms of a narrower ethos and thereby are transformed into something new. They are partial accretions, existing on the margins of mass culture and relying on the wealth and communications tools of a more homogenized center. Modernity continues to diminish the number of independent, totalizing worldviews.

We do see, however, that the Minerva phenomenon need not destroy the smaller culture forever and in all possible forms. After the passage of more time, the smaller culture often regroups and learns how to compete on the terms of the larger culture, leading to a cultural renaissance, albeit of a synthetic nature.

American Indian creativity, as illustrated by the Navajo, has made a comeback in recent decades, precisely through this mechanism. Many contemporary Navajo textiles, sandpaintings, and jewelry works sell for high prices and receive critical acclaim. The Navajo resurgence, however, has come under very different terms than the original Navajo successes. Navajo creators deal with the external marketplace in similar ways as do mainstream American artists. While trading posts survive for tourists, and sell many Navajo works, the best Navajo artists attach their names to original works of art, which they sell through galleries, most of all in Santa Fe. Most of the works are no longer explicitly ceremonial in nature. Navajo creators view themselves as independent artists with established individual reputations, and in this regard their ethos for the visual arts has become noticeably more Western. We have seen a Navajo cultural revival, but on terms that are partially Western rather than thoroughly Navajo in the earlier sense of that word.

## ▄ The Paradox of Diversity

If there is any contemporary ethos that is becoming predominant on a global scale, it is an ideology of individualistic self-fulfillment, bred through democracy, relatively free markets, and modern commercial society. This worldview takes many particular forms, but it is dominant or ascendant in the United States, Western Europe, and

Japan. Many of the lesser-developed countries, especially in Asia and Latin America, have been moving down a similar path. As Francis Fukuyama noted with his "end of history" thesis, this liberal-democratic worldview currently has no serious ideological competitor, even though dictatorships and anti-commercial polities remain.

The ethos of the contemporary world favors diversity in significant regards. A commercial society supports many differing styles and genres and creates a great number of artistic niches. It is no surprise that the United States provides such a wide range of offerings in fields as diverse as abstract art, popular music, jazz, contemporary classical music, cinema, poetry, architecture, biography, and both serious and blockbuster fiction, among many other areas. This diversity includes both the masterworks of the past and contemporary products.[20]

The diversity of modern commercial society nonetheless presents a paradox: a growing menu of choice in a particular society may limit the menu of choice for the world as a whole. As commercialism spreads, fewer societies will serve as a world apart from Western experience. Global production will yield only artistic outputs that come from a pro-diversity ethos.

Art collectors, sitting comfortably in American or European societies that already offer an amazing cornucopia of products, may not benefit much from the successful commercialization of Papua New Guinea. Such individuals might receive more from a Papua New Guinea where life is nasty, brutish, and short, akin to Hobbes's state of nature. Such a society, due to its profoundly different ethos, can produce cultural goods, such as intense tribal sculptures, that the developed West is lacking. Westerners can buy those goods, or at least view them in museums, without having to suffer the underlying costs of living in such societies.

Papua New Guinea is but a single example. Many renowned Third World and indigenous creations are rooted in cultures that

---

[20] See Cowen (1998) on this theme.

scorn and limit diversity, at least as we define that term in modern commercial society. The underlying ethoses in these societies are often based on illiberal religions, social practices, and political institutions. Many of their arts are closely tied to ceremonial and ritualistic functions and receive much of their vitality from these sources. Those arts and ceremonies would lose much of their importance if they had to compete for social loyalty in an unrestricted marketplace of ideas, replete with mass media, rock and roll, and Hollywood movies, not to mention Protestant and Mormon missionaries.

Commercialization will not dry up Third World and indigenous sources of creativity, but it will make them less uniquely specialized, at least relative to the already commercialized West. The world is losing many of the cultural products borne of anti-diversity ethoses, and for this reason we can never be fully happy with the consequences of cross-cultural exchange, no matter how great its triumphs. It is exactly the onset of a diverse menu of choice, and all of its concomitant benefits, that accounts for many of the tragic cultural losses in the world today.

# 4

### ▬ Why Hollywood Rules the World, and Whether We Should Care

Cinema is one of the hard cases for globalization. When we look at world music, the visual arts, or literature, it is readily apparent how trade has brought a more diverse menu of choice *and* helped many regions develop cultural identities. In each of these cultural sectors, the market has room for many producers, in large part because the costs of production are relatively low.

But what about film? In no other cultural area is America's export prowess so strong. Movies are very expensive to make, and in a given year there are far fewer films released than books, CDs, or paintings. These conditions appear to favor dominant producers at the expense of niche markets. So if cross-cultural exchange will look bad anywhere, it is in the realm of cinema.

Moviemaking also is prone to geographic clustering. Many cultural innovations and breakthroughs are spatially concentrated. If a good Italian Renaissance painter was not born in Florence, Venice, or Rome, he usually found it worthwhile to move to one of those locales. An analogous claim is true for Hollywood, which attracts cinematic talent from around the world, strengthening its market position.[1]

The degree of clustering has reached a sufficient extreme, and Hollywood movies have become so publicly visible, as to occasion charges of American cultural imperialism. European movies, in particular, have failed to penetrate global markets and also have lost ground at home. Many individuals claim that when it comes to cinema, global culture is a threat rather than a promise.

What lies behind these charges? To what extent is movie production clustered in Hollywood, and why has such clustering taken place? Why is European cinema so economically moribund? Have other national cinemas fared badly as well? Is cinematic clustering inimical to diversity, and if so, could it be reversed? Most generally, has cross-cultural exchange damaged diversity in the realm of cinema?

## ■ Why Clustering in Hollywood?

The current malaise in European cinema is driven by a concatenation of unfavorable forces, involving television, excess subsidies, demographics, language, the size of the American market, and Hollywood's more entrepreneurial environment. While some negative charges can be pinned on globalization, we will see that cross-cultural exchange is not the primary culprit in the story.

The United States has at least one natural advantage in moviemaking—it has the largest single home-market for cinema in dollar terms (although total attendance is higher in India). The countries that specialize in moviemaking will tend to be those countries where movies are most popular, in this case America and India. Hong Kong has been an exception to this principle, but a large domestic market does give a natural advantage. Home audiences often (though not always) prefer native products, if only for reasons of

---

[1] On cultural clustering generally, see Kroeber (1969); Porter (1990) and Hall (1998) provide a more modern treatment. The phenomenon was first noted by the Roman writer Velleius Paterculus (1967 [A.D. 30]).

language and cultural context, and this encourages production to shift to that market.

Aggregate market-size nonetheless remains only a single factor in determining who becomes a market leader. The United States, for instance, has been a large country for a long time, but only recently have European movies held such a low share of their home markets. In the mid-1960s, American films accounted for 35 percent of box office revenues in continental Europe; today the figure ranges between 80 to 90 percent. The greater population of the United States, and the greater American interest in moviegoing, do not themselves account for these changes.[2]

Furthermore, only certain kinds of cinema cluster in Hollywood. In a typical year the Western European nations make more movies than America does. In numeric terms most of the world's movies come from Asia, not from the United States. It is not unusual for India to release between 800 and 900 commercial films a year, compared to about 250 from the United States.[3]

The Hollywood advantage is concentrated in one very particular kind of moviemaking: films that are entertaining, highly visible, and have broad global appeal. The typical European film has about 1 percent of the audience of the typical Hollywood film, and this differential has been growing. American movies have become increasingly popular in international markets, while European movies have become less so.[4]

Not surprisingly, the Europeans invest less money in each film than do Hollywood producers. One estimate from the early 1990s placed the average European film budget at $3 million and the average American budget at $11 million. The average film budget for a major Hollywood studio (as opposed to an independent studio) has been estimated at $34 million. These numbers omit marketing and audience research budgets, the area where American moviemakers outspend their European counterparts most. For an average Holly-

---

[2] On the increase of American revenue in Europe, see Puttnam (1998, p. 266).
[3] On western Europe, see Ilott (1996, p. 14).
[4] On the growing differential, see Dale (1997, p. 119).

wood movie, domestic and foreign marketing expenditures might run at least $30 million. European estimates are hard to find, in part because the numbers are so small and not susceptible to easy measurement.[5] The question is not why Hollywood makes more movies than Europe, because it does not. The question is why Hollywood movies have more global export success, while European movies are aimed at small but guaranteed local audiences.

As recently as 1985, French movies outgrossed the Hollywood product in their home market. Since that time, Hollywood's ability to capture so much of French film revenue (often up to 80 percent) has come largely because French revenues have declined, not because Hollywood revenues have risen so much.[6]

The turning point in this dynamic appears to have started in the 1970s. Before the 1970s, most national European cinemas still experienced a significant degree of export success, whatever problems the industry as a whole had. Since that time, European moviemakers have seen their export markets collapse. In essence, Hollywood is now competing with the native European producers in each individual country, rather than with cross-European exports.

The popularization of television, and the timing of this popularization, damaged European cinema. As television became widespread throughout Europe, movie audiences dwindled. In Germany, 800 million movie tickets were bought in 1956, but only 180 million were bought in 1962. At the same time, the number of television sets rose from 700,000 to 7.2 million. In the U.K., cinematic attendance fell from 292 million in 1967 to 73 million in 1986. In France, movie attendance dropped from 450 million in 1956 to 122 million in 1988. In Japan, the number of movie tickets sold in 1985 was only a sixth of what it had been twenty-five years earlier. The cataclysmic nature of these shocks should not be underestimated.[7]

[5] See Ilott (1996, p. 27), and Dale (1997, p. 31).

[6] Segrave (1997, p. 270), and Pells (1997, p. 275).

[7] See Kaes (1997, p. 614), Dunnett (1990, p. 43), Noam (1991, p. 59), and Dissanayake (1988, p. 16).

This negative demand shock forced European moviemaking to contract. Hollywood stepped into the void, just as it did during and after the First World War, an earlier crisis period for European cinema. Hollywood became strongest when European competitors were most vulnerable.

American moviemakers had experienced a similar audience crisis, but much earlier, due to the more rapid spread of television in the United States. Television became common in the United States ten or more years before it did in Europe. The U.S. film audience declined by 50 percent, but this happened over the 1946–1956 period rather than later, as in Europe. By 1955, two-thirds of all American households already had television sets.[8]

Hollywood responded actively to this challenge. Starting as early as the 1950s, American moviemakers responded to television by making high-stakes, risky investments in marketing, glamour, and special effects. In the 1960s American directors found greater latitude to experiment with sex and violence; this trend was formalized with the abandonment of the Hays Code in 1966. By the 1970s, Hollywood movies had become significantly more exciting to mass audiences than they had been a decade before. *Jaws* and *Star Wars* were emblematic of this new era. Hollywood was ready to move in with innovative products, expressly designed to compete with television. At exactly the same time, the European moviemakers found themselves unable to compete with television, and reeling from this very strong negative shock. For Hollywood it turned out to be a blessing in disguise that television hit the American market first.

Demographics have worsened the problems of European moviemakers. In most countries, individuals older than thirty-five no longer go to movies in significant numbers, preferring instead to watch television. Moviegoing is the province of the young. Most European countries suffer twice here. First, they have older populations than does the United States. Second, the traditional "art

[8] See Rifkin (2000, p. 25) on the timing of the decline in America. On the 1955 statistic, see Caves (2000, p. 94).

house" styles of European film are better suited to old audiences than to young ones. This makes them especially hard to export. The advent of the cinematic multiplex, which tends to attract the young to movies more than the old, has reinforced these problems.

A self-reinforcing dynamic has since expanded Hollywood's export advantage. American success has led to easier finance and greater marketing expenditures, which in turn has led to greater export potential. Hollywood films have become successively more global, while European films target small but guaranteed revenue sources, such as state subsidies, or television rights, sold to government-regulated stations. A vicious circle has been created: the more European producers fail in global markets, the more they rely on television revenue and subsidies. The more they rely on television and subsidies, the more they fail in global markets.

Television has cut into the American and European cinematic markets in different fashion. Video rentals are a more important income source in the American market, whereas the sale of television rights plays a bigger role in most of Western Europe.

U.S. figures (circa 1993), place pay and free television at 19 percent of cinematic revenues, movie theaters at 27 percent, and home video at 49 percent. In contrast, television receipts account for more than half of film revenue in the French market. Not every European country exhibits the same dependence on television, but France is by far the biggest movie producer in Europe and accounts for roughly half of all West European movie output by dollar value.[9] The problems of European cinema are, in large part, the problems of French cinema.

The revenue reliance on broadcast television makes European movies less suited for the export market. Television provides a largely passive audience. Many TV viewers turn on the set and watch whatever is on, without paying serious attention to the program. They do little to enforce high standards of quality production. Production for the television market tends towards the mundane

[9] Ilott (1996, pp. 10, 27, passim).

and the formulaic. Glitzy special effects are rare. We find these same features in made-for-TV films in the United States. A few of these films are excellent (such as Steven Spielberg's early *Duel*), but most are undistinguished and boring, despite the immense talent in Hollywood. Most of all, made-for-TV movies are not well suited for export to large audiences. In essence, Europe simply has more made-for-TV movies than the United States, regardless of the claimed pretense of theatrical release.

The home video market, more prominent in the United States, is more competitive and demanding than television, and imposes greater discipline on the moviemaker. The customers must be impelled to go out and rent a movie in the first place. Then they must choose a particular film from among hundreds or thousands of competing titles in the video store. The U.S. also has a more competitive television market, due to the larger number of cable channels, which requires that video rentals meet higher quality standards.

In the United States, the television and video markets serve as handmaidens for the theatrical market, augmenting its influence over the quality of the product. While some movies succeed on video alone, video success typically depends on the advance publicity generated by the film at the theatrical box office. The same can be said for success on television, or for the sale of television rights. Theatrical revenue thus drives both video revenue and television revenue in the American market. In Europe, in contrast, television revenue is more likely to be a *substitute* for theatrical revenue. European films, which experience major box office successes far less frequently, are more likely to be placed on television as filler.

The roles of television and subsidies are closely linked. Most west European nations have television stations that are owned, controlled, or strictly regulated by their respective governments, which use them to promote a national cultural agenda. Typically the stations face domestic-content restrictions, must spend a certain percentage of revenue on domestic films, must operate a film production subsidiary, or they willfully overpay for films for political reasons. The end result is overpayment for broadcast rights—the most important subsidy that many European moviemakers receive. Audience levels are typically no more than one or two million at the television level, even in the larger countries such as France—too small to justify the sums paid to moviemakers for television rights on economic grounds.[10]

European films receive many other forms of subsidy. In France, for instance, direct subsidies are available from the national government, regional governments, European subsidy bodies (such as Eurimages) and coproduction subsidies through other national governments. Often French producers need only put up 15 percent of the budget of their films to receive subsidies. French producers also receive "Sofica" tax shelters (estimated worth of more than 5 percent of total budgets), automatic box office aid from the government (estimated at 7.7 percent of total budget), a discretionary subsidy called *avance sur recettes*, which takes the form of an interest-free loan (estimated at over 5 percent of total budget), and subsidies for the promotion of French films abroad. A 1970 study estimated that 60 percent of the avance subsidy was in fact never recovered. Money is also advanced for the development of new film ideas, and for script rewriting, if the proposed film is rejected when it applies for subsidies on the first go-round. There is a special subsidy fund for coproductions with east European filmmakers. The French government also subsidizes the upkeep and construction of cinemas—an indirect subsidy to moviemakers—and encourages French banks to lend money to moviemaking projects. A number of other French institutions are not formally state-controlled but act in conjunction with the state system, subsidizing scriptwriters, directors, and production companies.[11]

Martin Dale, a cinema industry analyst, has estimated that the state provides at least 70 *percent* of the funding for the average conti-

---

[10] For details on European television regulations, see Grantham (2000, chap. 4), Dale (1997, p. 119), and Noam (1991, pp. 107, 112).

[11] On the 1970 study, see French Ministry of Culture (1970, p. 45). For a more general list and outlining of these subsidies, see Wangermee (1991) and "International Film Finance," at http://forth.stir.ac.uk/~fmzpl1/France.html. On some details about German subsidies, see Kolmel (1985).

nental film, taking all subsidies into account. This figure is speculative rather than exact, if only because the wide variety of subsidy schemes, and their complex nature, makes their final impact difficult to trace. Nonetheless subsidy-granting bodies provide more than supplemental assistance for European moviemakers; rather, they have become the primary customer.[12]

Subsidies encourage producers to serve domestic demand and the wishes of politicians and cinematic bureaucrats, rather than produce movies for international export. Many films will be made, even when they have little chance of turning a profit in stand-alone terms. The film industries will not develop specialized talents in demand forecasting and marketing, as Hollywood has done.

The training of cinematic talent in the United States and Europe reflects these differences. American film schools are like business schools in many regards. European film schools have become more like humanities programs, emphasizing semiotics, critical theory, and contemporary left-wing philosophies. The European directors that survive tend to be established and to have longstanding political connections; one 1995 study estimated that 85 percent of the film directors in France were over fifty years of age at the time. The younger talents set their sights on Hollywood from the beginning, rather than staying at home to develop a domestic cinema.[13]

The two non-Hollywood cinemas that have enjoyed the most export success—India and Hong Kong—are run on an explicitly commercial basis. Some segments of the Indian film industry receive government subsidies, but the overwhelming majority of new releases do not. They are commercial productions made for profit and frequently exported abroad, usually to other underdeveloped nations but often to the United Kingdom as well. By numerous measures, such as attendance or number of films released, the Indian movie industry is the largest and the most successful in the world. Indian movies are frequently criticized for their generic nature or

[12] See Dale (1997, p. 123).
[13] On film school, see Dale (1997, pp. 206–7). On the age of directors, see Micklethwait and Wooldridge (2000, p. 199), and Dale (1997, p. 161).

sappy plots, but in terms of music, cinematography, and use of color, they are often quite beautiful and even pathbreaking compared to Western productions.

The Hong Kong film industry has experienced export success from the 1970s onward, mostly throughout Southeast Asia. At its peak it released more films per year than any Western country, and as an exporter it was second only to the United States. Furthermore, Hong Kong cinema arose in a market that was dominated by Hollywood up through the late 1960s. In the 1970s and 1980s, however, Hollywood sometimes failed to capture even 30 percent of the domestic Hong Kong market. Only since 1997, when Hong Kong returned to China, did Hollywood movies take in more than half of the total local box office.[14]

At first Hong Kong movies focused on the martial arts, but they subsequently branched out to include police movies, romance, comedy, horror, and ghost stories, among other genres. The best of these movies, such as John Woo's *The Killer*, or *Hardboiled*, are acclaimed as high art and have had considerable influence on directors around the world. David Bordwell, in his recent *Planet Hong Kong*, claimed, "Since the 1970s it has been arguably the world's most energetic, imaginative popular cinema." Hong Kong movies are made on a commercial basis and have received no government assistance. In recent times, however, the industry has been damaged by the Chinese takeover of Hong Kong and by fears of censorship.[15]

Many of the complaints about American cultural imperialism have an excessively Eurocentric slant. Today's mainstream European cinema does appear less creative and less vital than its 1950–1970 heyday. But by most common critical standards, cinematic creativity has risen in Taiwan, China, Iran, South Korea, the Philippines, Latin America, and many parts of Africa, among other locales. Even within Europe, the creative decline is restricted to a few of the larger nations, such as France and Italy. Danish cinema is more influential and more successful today than in times past, and arguably the same

---

[14] On Hong Kong cinema, see Bordwell (2000, pp. 1, 34, passim).
[15] See Bordwell (2000, p. 1).

is true for Spanish cinema as well. Mexican and Argentinean film-makers are enjoying a resurgence. While these producers all struggle against Hollywood competition, creative world-filmmaking is not on a downward trajectory.

## ■ The English Language, and the Move from Silents to Talkies

The English language, combined with America's role as world leader, has strengthened Hollywood exports. Cinematic clustering, and the current crisis of European cinema, is rooted partially in the transition from silent film to talkies.

Counterintuitively, the onset of the sound era increased Hollywood's share of world cinematic revenue. At the time of the transition, equipping the theaters with sound and making movies with sound were costly. To recoup these costs, theaters sought out high-quality, high-expenditure productions for large audiences. The small, cheap, quick film became less profitable, given the suddenly higher fixed costs of production and presentation. This shift in emphasis favored Hollywood moviemakers over their foreign competitors.[16]

More generally, the higher the fixed costs of production, the greater the importance of drawing a large audience and the greater the importance of demand forecasting and marketing. Today costly special effects and expensive celebrity stars drive the push for block-busters in similar fashion, and favor Hollywood production as well.

The talkies, by introducing issues of translation, boosted the dominant world language of English and thus benefited Hollywood. Given the growing importance of English as a world language, and the focal importance of the United States, European countries would sooner import films from Hollywood than from each other. A multiplicity of different cultures or languages often favors the relative position of the dominant one, which becomes established as a common standard of communication. During the si-

[16] Segrave (1997, p. 74; Usabel 1982, pp. 80–82).

lent era, in contrast, European films enjoyed an even footing in the export market, as language was not an issue.

Hollywood executives properly regarded the onset of talkies as an opportunity to expand abroad, rather than as a reason for trepidation. At the time of the transition, some movie executives speculated that talking pictures would make English the language of the entire world, which has turned out to be only a partial exaggeration of the truth.[17]

Once America, and the English language, became established as a world standard, this proved self-reinforcing. American audiences, the world's largest moviegoing audience at the time, became accustomed to seeing films in their native language. Dubbed or subtitled movies have a difficult time in the United States to this day, whereas most other audiences accept them with few complaints. In Germany, the individuals who dub the German-language voices of prominent American actors and actresses can become celebrities in their own right, if their manner of speech is sufficiently memorable. Dubbers become known as the German voice of John Wayne, Tom Hanks, or Jack Nicholson.

This difference in linguistic expectations means that European moviemakers have a much harder time penetrating the American market than vice versa. The American export advantage is based on a combination of outward-looking producers and inward-looking consumers.

The move to sound, and the rise of English as an export standard, provided a strong boost to the movie exports of Great Britain. While the U.K. has never seriously rivaled Hollywood as a moviemaking power, many U.K. releases have succeeded on a global scale, essentially by mimicking the Hollywood style. The James Bond movies and David Lean's *Lawrence of Arabia* or *Bridge over River Kwai* are some of the best-known British successes.[18]

---

[17] Crafton (1997, p. 422). In particular sectors or times when the American market-share fell, other events appear to have operated, such as trade quotas, patent problems, or the Great Depression (Crafton 1997, chap. 17; Thompson 1985, pp. 164–65).

[18] See, for instance, Puttnam (1998, p. 113) on how sound boosted the English export sectors in its early years.

Today the United Kingdom is the leading European exporter of movies to other European nations. In 1991, the U.K. put out 36 movies, 56 percent of which were exported to France. In the same year, France put out 140 movies, only 14 percent of which were exported to the U.K. Italy, Spain, and Germany have export performances that are far worse than the French record. Not surprisingly, U.K. moviemakers spend more per film than anywhere else in Europe and rely less on subsidies than their continental counterparts. U.K. producers also have been geared to export for a long time. Given how much of their home market is captured by Hollywood, U.K. features must reap export revenue to turn a profit.[19]

We see tendencies towards a common linguistic standard in other cinematic markets as well. Throughout the Arabic world numerous dialects are spoken. This has helped Cairo, through the use of Egyptian Arabic, to attain a position as the dominant movie exporter to other Arabic nations. Egyptian Arabic is now widely understood around the Arabic world, in large part because non-Egyptians receive so many movies and television programs in the language. This audience is now more likely to patronize the Egyptian product, which makes it harder for other Arab nations to compete. India has fifteen languages and two thousand dialects, but the Hindi cinema of Bombay dominates cross-regional exports within India. While more films are made in Madras and other locales, Bombay films command most of the investment, attract the biggest stars, have the greatest national following, and have the greatest success internationally, usually in other Third World countries. The Philippines has many languages as well, but Tagalog has priority in the world of cinema. These forms of national and regional segmentation illustrate the tendency for a dominant cinematic language, just as do global markets.[20]

The move to talkies provides a natural "controlled experiment" to isolate the importance of language. In the silent era, of course, the language of a movie simply was not an issue.

---

[19] Ilott (1996, pp. 14, 28).

[20] On Bombay dominance, see Chakravarty (1993, p. 44), Gokulsing and Dissanayake (1998, p. 123), and Lent (1990, p. 231).

In essence, talkies made it easier for non-Hollywood producers to capture part of their home markets, but made it harder for them to export abroad. European movies commanded a greater share of their respective home markets in the 1930s, compared to the silent era. The domestic market offered a certain percentage of "captive" viewers who preferred their native language. So European movie-makers turned their attention inward, given the greater ease of pleasing the home market and the greater difficulty of exporting.

French film production doubled between 1928 to 1938, and French movies commanded over half of their domestic market throughout the 1930s. In 1936 the six most popular French films were all native French products. Of the seventy-five most popular films, fifty-six were French, as opposed to fifteen from America. In 1935, 70 percent of all film receipts in France went to French-pro-duced movies. In comparison, in 1925, at the height of the silent era, American exports accounted for 70 percent of the French market.[21]

The sound era offered the greatest relative benefits to the na-tional cinemas that were not exporting much in the first place. The export promise of these products, relative to Hollywood, could not fall, since it was close to zero in the first place. Cinema blossomed in Hungary, the Netherlands, Norway, Mexico, and Czechoslovakia, among other places, at least relative to the silent era. The Hong Kong cinema started in the 1930s, and used the Cantonese dialect as its primary selling point in southern China. In contrast, Sweden and Denmark, which were significant movie exporters in the silent era, did not fare nearly as well with the onset of talkies.[22]

The sound era also transformed movies through the introduc-tion of recorded musical soundtracks. In the 1920s, foreign films, mostly American, captured approximately 85 percent of the Indian

[21] See Crisp (1993, p. 12), Andrew (1983, p. 57), Hayes (1930, pp. 194–95), and Sklar (1975, p. 222). Quotas limited American films to seven-eighths of the market, which was more than the American share had ever been. On 1925, see Magder (1993, p. 21), and Costigliola (1984, p. 176). The French market offers the clearest field for compari-son, given the rise of fascism in Germany and Italy, and accompanying restrictions on foreign films.

[22] See Armes (1987, p. 63), Dibbets (1997, p. 219), Schnitman (1984, p. 15), and Teo (1997, pp. 6–7).

market. By the end of the 1930s, this had fallen to 20 percent. In the new sound era, film music was a greater lure for Indian audiences than dialogue, and arguably remains so to this day. Hollywood has no comparative advantage at producing high-quality Indian popular music. Indian producers marketed their films domestically on the basis of their music, and quickly developed new centers of cinematic production in Bombay, Calcutta, and Madras.[23]

Music provided a similar protective role in Argentina, where hundreds of musical comedies were made in the early years of sound. The Argentinean Carlos Gardel, more of a tango singer than an actor, became the hottest Latin cinematic star of this era. Hollywood has never had a strong comparative advantage in producing musicals for foreign audiences, and its international influence has been limited accordingly. The general decline of the musical, however, has weakened an area where national cinemas traditionally held their own against Hollywood imports.[24]

## ▬ The Drive towards Clustering

In part, movie production clusters in particular geographic areas simply because there is no reason *not* to have clustering. When the cost of shipping the relevant goods and services are low, clustering makes economic sense.

Consider a more general economic analogy. There is more trade and mobility across the United States of America than across the disparate countries of Western Europe. This trade causes the economic profiles of the American states to diverge.

In economic terms, the countries of Western Europe are more likely to resemble each other than are the American states. Most of the American states have no steel industry, no automobile industry, and no wheat industry; instead they buy the products of these in-

---

[23] On these points, see Barnouw and Krishnaswamy (1963, p. 39), Sklar (1975, p. 226), Baskaran (1981, p. 99), and Armes (1987, p. 62). On musicals in Egypt, see Khan (1969, pp. 23–30).

[24] On Gardel, see John King (1990, p. 37), and Schnitman (1984, p. 54).

dustries from other states or countries. But typically a nation of western Europe has its own steel, automobile, dairy, and agriculture sectors, largely because of subsidies and protectionism. Free trade within the United States allows states and regions to specialize to a high degree and causes their economic profiles to diverge; in a freer economic environment, the economies of western Europe would take the same path.[25]

Trade and specialization thus bring geographic clustering when the basic product is mobile. Most American peanuts are grown in Georgia and Virginia and then shipped to the rest of the country. In contrast, each region of the United States performs its own cement manufacture, as does each country. The costs of trading and transporting cement are too high for clustered production, and subsequent transport, to be feasible. Action movies, however, resemble peanuts more than cement in this regard, especially if the film appeals broadly to many cultural groups.

Some of Hollywood's cinematic clustering is driven by the short-run, dynamic nature of film projects. Studios may dally over projects for years, but once the go-ahead decision has been made, the moviemakers wish to move as quickly as possible, to meet a perceived market demand. They need to assemble a large number of skilled employees on very short notice, and therefore they will "fish" for talent in a common, clustered pool. In similar fashion, the computer industry changes rapidly, many projects are short term, and once a go-ahead decision has been made, large numbers of talented employees must be assembled rapidly. Common forces therefore shape the clusters of Silicon Valley and Hollywood.

It is not always the case that movies can be *filmed* more cheaply in Hollywood than elsewhere. In fact, Hollywood studio hands are worried about how many movies are being outsourced to Canada, Australia, and other non-U.S. locales, to lower production costs. Rather, clustering eases the finding, lining up, and evaluating of the movie's critical assets, such as stars, directors, and screenplays.

---

[25] Note that clustering will tend to maintain distinct regional ethoses as well, by giving each area a different economic and thus social flavor.

These tasks are still done in Hollywood rather than in Vancouver or Sydney, regardless of where the movie is filmed.

The Hollywood cluster has a superior ability to evaluate cinematic projects and, in particular, to forecast and meet consumer demand. Hollywood is the geographic center for these kinds of talent. Ironically, it is easier to get a film made in Europe than America. In Hollywood, studios scrutinize projects intensely and refuse to finance projects that do not have a good chance of commercial success. Most European moviemakers do not apply similar filters. Hollywood is a cluster, in part, for the same reasons that New York and London are clustered banking centers. In both cases talents for large-scale project evaluation gravitate towards a single geographic area.[26]

Moviemaking has become more expensive over the last thirty years, due largely to special effects, rising celebrity salaries, and marketing expenditures. All of these features have increased the natural advantage of talents for demand forecasting and project evaluation. They have increased the natural advantage of Hollywood.

Initial clusters often generate snowball effects, attracting yet more talent to the commercial center. When European directors want to make popular movies, they now go to Hollywood, as we have seen with Ridley Scott, Paul Verhoeven, Bernardo Bertolucci, and Jean-Jacques Annaud, among many others. Initial differences thus become self-cumulating rather than self-reversing.

For this reason, one "turnaround" event can shift a cluster from one locale to another. In the case of cinema, the French lost their dominant market position only with the First World War, which caused the major combatants to virtually cease film production for four years. Hollywood stepped into the vacuum and first penetrated world markets on a large scale in the 1920s. The snowball effect shifted the direction of its momentum, and the United States rapidly surpassed the French as the world's largest movie exporter in only a few year's time after the First World War.[27]

---

[26] The above analysis draws on Ilott (1996).

[27] See Krugman (1979, 1980) on the operation of snowball effects.

# ■ Clustering Myths

A common myth is that America dominates world cinematic markets because of its monopoly power. Yet all the primary distributors in Europe are owned by European media groups and regulated by European governments. When the Cineplex Odeon movie theater chain in the United States was Canadian-owned, and for a while jointly Canadian- and British-owned, it made little difference on the screen.

A second myth is that Hollywood dominates because it can sell its movies so cheaply abroad, having recovered their costs in the home market. The claim is that the movie can be dumped abroad, since "it has already been paid for."

This argument does not provide the fundamental reason for America's market share. At most it explains why Hollywood films are booked by cinemas, not why they are so popular with audiences. When European consumers choose whether to see an American or an indigenous production, typically the ticket prices are the same or roughly the same (if anything the American movie might be more costly, all things considered, given time spent waiting in line). The American dominance arises because at equal admission prices, European consumers prefer to see American movies.

If the critics are correct that Hollywood's fundamental advantage is on the cost side for film rentals, we should observe relatively empty theaters for American films in Europe. The cheapness of Hollywood films would cause so many films to be imported that the marginal Hollywood film would draw a small audience. (To consider a limiting case, if it cost nothing to show a Hollywood film, so many would be imported that they would play even to virtually empty theaters.) Those films would be carried primarily for their cheapness, not for their popularity. But we do not observe this outcome. When American movies are shown in Europe, the critics complain that the theaters are full. If Hollywood dominated the market on cost grounds, rather than on popularity grounds, Europeans would not fear cultural imperialism as they do.

The argument that Hollywood movies have "already been paid for" has another logical flaw. Movies from all countries have already been paid for, once they are made. The fundamental issue is what gets made in the first place, and what then gets shown abroad, and that depends on consumer demand. So many Hollywood movies are made, and with such high levels of funding and marketing, because they can draw large audiences.[28]

Similar points apply to many media industries, such as when Canadians claim that America dump television shows or magazines at very low cost, since the producers are already making a profit in the U.S. market. But again, we typically do not observe American products preferred for their cheapness, we observe them preferred for their superiority in entertaining the audience.

The correct version of the argument notes that suppliers with a large home or captive market often can afford to make better products. Given their larger built-in audience, they can invest more money in quality, and earn the investment back on ticket sales more easily. Films from Burkina Faso do not have expensive special effects. This argument, however, leads us back to the conclusion that the more expensive movies are better movies, at least in the eyes of the audience, if not always in more objective aesthetic terms.

If we examine the television market, the dumping argument implies an irony. To the extent that Hollywood TV programs or movie rights have been sold cheaply in Europe, it is because European TV stations have held a strong bargaining position (a "monopsony," in economic language). Until the recent partial deregulation of European television, the number of program buyers in a single country has sometimes been as small as one or two government-owned or government-controlled channels. The single buyer, through bargaining, could limit the price paid for rights to a Hollywood movie. Ironically, the cheap sale of Hollywood movies to television has, in

[28] We do find some times when American films are plentiful in a country but do not draw so many viewers. Germany in the 1950s provides one example (Garncarz 1994, p. 101), but this case is an exception to the general state of affairs. For other criticisms of this explanation for Hollywood domination, see Noam (1991, pp. 12–20).

the past, subsidized the state-controlled, noncommercial products of European television.[29] Without monopsony, the price of movie rights would be bid up to reflect the potential popularity of the movie.

Note that America has had much less success in exporting its television programs than its movies, despite having the largest domestic television market in the world. The popularity of domestic television programs is robust; even the African nations command a reasonable share of their domestic television market. While some American shows have been exported successfully, they are not hits in every country; *Dallas* was a failure in Brazil and Japan. American television programs show no sign of taking over the world, and in many countries they are losing market share. In 1998, for instance, American television programs were unable to crack the top ten in any of the major Western European markets.[30]

In part, television programs face a more passive audience and need not meet the exacting technical standards of the cinematic medium. Hollywood has never had a strong comparative advantage at producing relatively low-cost drama. In some genres, such as the soap opera, Brazil and Mexico have proven more effective exporters than the United States, again showing the special and limited nature of the Hollywood advantage in international markets.[31]

America cannot even dominate the market for Spanish-language Latin television, even though the 30 million or so Latins in the United States are the single largest Latin audience in terms of purchasing power. The Miami-based stations of Television and Unimundo import most of their dramatic programs from Mexico and South America, rather than making them in the United States. As a result, some U.S. Latins have objected to the "cultural imperialism" behind this practice, wishing instead for a home-grown Miami product.[32]

---

[29] Noam (1991, p. 20).

[30] Micklethwait and Woolridge (2000, p. 194).

[31] On the lesser American success in exporting television, see Negrine and Papathanassopoulos (1990, p. 160), Dunnett (1990, pp. 41, 194–95), Allen (1996, p. 123), and Berwanger (1995, pp. 316–17).

[32] On the Latin market, see Navarro (2000).

## ▰ American Cultural Imperialism?

When Hollywood penetrates global markets, to what extent is *American* culture being exported? Or is a new global culture being created, above and beyond its specifically American origins? There is no simple answer to this question.

Critics of cultural imperialism make two separate and partially contradictory charges. Some are unhappy with the global spread of the American ethos of commercialism and individualism. Other complaints focus on the strong global-market position of a relatively universal cultural product, rather than local products based on national or particularist inspirations. There is some truth to each complaint, although they point in opposite directions.

If we look at the national identities of the major individuals involved, Hollywood is highly cosmopolitan. Many of the leading Hollywood directors are non-Americans by birth, including Ridley Scott (British) and James Cameron (Canadian), who were among the hottest Hollywood directors circa 2001. Arnold Schwarzenegger, Charlie Chaplin, and Jim Carrey have been among the leading non-American U.S. stars. Most of the major studios are now foreign owned. A typical production will have Sony, a Japanese company, hire a European director to shoot a picture in Canada and then sell the product for global export. Of the world's major entertainment corporations, only Time-Warner is predominantly American in ownership.

For better or worse, Hollywood strives to present the universal to global audiences. As Hollywood markets its films to more non-English speakers, those films become more general. Action films are favored over movies with subtle dialogue. Comedy revolves around slapstick rather than verbal puns. The larger the audience, of course, the more universal the product or celebrity must be. There is relatively little that the world as a whole, or even a select group of fifty million global consumers, can agree on. Greater universality means that the movies are relevant to general features of the human condition, but it also can bring blandness and formulaic treatment. Critics allege that American culture is driving the world, but in reality the two are determined simultaneously, and by the same set of forces.

Non-American movies, when they pursue foreign markets, must strive for universality as well. The Jackie Chan Hong Kong movie *Rumble in the Bronx* was marketed in the United States with success. The producers, however, cut parts of the movie to appeal to American audiences. All of the action sequences were kept, but the relationship of Chan with the co-star was diminished, in part because the woman (Anita Mui) was a star in Asia but not in the United States, and in part because the relationship was based on the "Chinese" values of obligation and loyalty, rather than on a Western sense of erotic romance.[33]

The most successful Canadian cultural export is the Harlequin romance novel. In 1990 Harlequin sold more than 200 million books, accounting for 40 percent (!) of all mass-market paperback sales in the United States. This fact is rarely cited by Canadian critics of American cultural imperialism, largely because this export success does not "count" for them. The Harlequin romance does not reflect a specifically Canadian perspective, whatever that designation might mean, but rather targets a broad circle of female readers.[34]

Despite these powerful universalist forces, the American and national component to Hollywood moviemaking cannot be ignored. Hollywood has always drawn on the national ethos of the United States for cinematic inspiration. The American values of heroism, individualism, and romantic self-fulfillment are well suited for the large screen and for global audiences. It is true that Hollywood will make whatever will sell abroad. Nonetheless, *how well* Hollywood can make movies in various styles will depend on native sources of inspiration. Hollywood has an intrinsic cost-advantage in making movies based upon American values, broadly construed, and thus has an intrinsic advantage in exporting such movies. The clustering

[33] See Fore (1997, p. 250).

[34] On Cineplex Odeon, see Gomery (1992, p. 105). On the history of Harlequin, see Twitchell (1992, pp. 92–93. On the Canadian nature of Harlequin, see Audley (1983, pp. 101, 107).

of filmmaking in Hollywood cannot help but be based on an partially American ethos.

For this reason, dominant cultures, such as the United States,
have an advantage in exporting their values and shaping the preferences of other nations. Consider food markets. Many Third World
citizens like to eat at McDonald's, not just because the food tastes
good to them, but also because McDonald's is a visible symbol of
the West and the United States. When they walk through the doors
of a McDonald's, they are entering a different world. The McDonald's corporation, knowing this, designs its Third World interiors to
reflect the glamour of Western commerce, much as a shopping mall
would. McDonald's shapes its product to meet global demands, but
builds on the American roots of the core concept. The McDonald's
image and product lines have been refined in the American domestic market and draw heavily on American notions of the relation
between food and social life.

The promulgated American ethos will, of course, successfully
meld both national and cosmopolitan influences, and will not be
purely American in any narrow sense. American cinema, like American cuisine, has been a synthetic, polyglot product from the beginning. Hollywood was developed largely by foreigners—Jewish immigrants from Eastern Europe—and was geared towards
entertaining American urban audiences, which were drawn from
around the world.

Furthermore, Hollywood's universality has, in part, *become* a
central part of American national culture. Commercial forces have
led America to adopt "that which can be globally sold" as part of
its national culture. Americans have decided to emphasize their international triumphs and their ethnic diversity as part of their national self-image. In doing so, Americans have, to some extent,
traded away particularist strands of their culture for success in
global markets.

In this regard Hollywood's global-market position is a Faustian
bargain. Achieving global dominance requires a sacrifice of a culture's initial perspective to the demands of world consumers. Amer-

ican culture is being exported, but for the most part it is not Amish quilts and Herman Melville. *Jurassic Park*, a movie about dinosaurs, was a huge hit abroad, but *Forrest Gump*, which makes constant reference to American history and national culture, made most of its money at home.

## ▰ The Virtues of Living at the Margins

Hollywood's export success shapes the cinematic market. First and most prominently, it finances spectacular, blockbuster productions. While many of these productions are aesthetically mediocre, others are excellent, though few critics agree on which are the good ones. Clearly, to the extent we use audience preferences as the relevant standard of value, Hollywood succeeds.

In addition to these blockbusters, the financial success of the industry supports diversity. Not all Hollywood products fit the "least common denominator" model. Hollywood puts out a wide range of independent releases, creative comedies, and films that do not fit any easily identifiable category. The late 1990s have in particular were renowned for the wide variety of high quality, non-mainstream fare coming out of Hollywood.

"Microbudget" films are far more common in the United States than in Europe. A microbudget film is one made by a previously amateur director on a minuscule budget, typically less than $100,000. Among the best-known microfilms are Spike Lee's *She's Gotta Have It*, the Coen brothers' *Blood Simple*, and *The Blair Witch Project*. All of these innovative projects have been made under director control and liberated from the constraints of studio production.

It is no accident that Hollywood has both the largest studio apparatus and the greatest number of microbudget films. Building a film industry of any kind requires a regular supply of popular product. A healthy commercial base is needed to support an infrastructure of theaters, production companies, film schools, and marketing institutions. Independent or innovative filmmakers benefit from this infrastructure just as the major studios do.

The major studios typically seek to buy out and "corrupt" the independent filmmakers, and in this sense the two cinematic worlds are always at war with each other. But in a larger sense they are complements. The mainstream desire to commercialize the independents helps finance their existence. Directors invest their money in microbudget films in part because they have a chance of receiving a subsequent contract from a major studio. Such contracts bring both money and the resources to film their larger visions. In addition to the Coen brothers and Spike Lee, Francis Coppola, Peter Bogdanovich, Martin Scorsese, Jonathan Demme, David Lynch, Sam Raimi, John Sayles, and Jim Jarmusch all first made their names with microbudget films. The directors of *The Blair Witch Project* were courted for a Hollywood sequel, which earned them millions, despite its low quality. Hollywood studios, whatever their conservatism and their flaws, are always looking for the "next hot thing." If they can find a microbudget production that is marketable, they will seek to co-opt it, but in the meantime they are providing the "prizes" that drive the independent market.

European studios, in contrast, never expect high returns from projects, and thus they adopt a more conservative attitude. Notable European directors such as Godard, Bertolucci, Truffaut, Besson, and Pasolini found their start with microbudget films, but the overall commercial weakness of European cinema is making those kinds of opportunities harder to find and exploit.[35]

It is not altogether bad that European cinema lacks the export promise of Hollywood. While commercial improvement would undoubtedly benefit European cinema, diversity would not be served by a fully "level playing field" in the industry. The dirty little secret of today's cinematic world is the following: the very features of the film industry behind American export dominance also have supported diversity of style around the globe.

The global prowess of Hollywood means that European moviemakers pursue different markets and produce different kinds of cre-

[35] See Dale (1997, p. 243).

ativity. Many of the interesting qualities of European movies come precisely from their *inability* to reach world markets on a large scale. Shut out of world markets, European movies have been able to focus on nuances of language and culture. They typically do not have happy but superficial endings, opting, rather, for something more interesting. The non-Hollywood productions that have success abroad, such as *Four Weddings and a Funeral* or *Like Water for Chocolate*, often have many of the flaws that plague mainstream Hollywood releases: saccharine, cliched characters or an unrealistically happy ending.

European pictures from the silent era, which had a greater chance of export success, were more like the American movies of their time than are current European productions, or European films of the 1950s or 1960s. European talkies, because they are aimed at different audience segments, have not followed the same artistic path as Hollywood. Hollywood's asymmetric economic strength, while it comes under heavy criticism, in fact supports aesthetic diversity.

Similarly, the creativity of Hong Kong moviemaking in the 1980s would not have been possible had those pictures been geared to export to American and Europe, rather than the smaller and more specialized Southeast Asian market. The Hong Kong movie *Dr. Lamb* was a success in the Hong Kong market of the 1990s. The movie was explicitly patterned after *Silence of the Lambs*, a U.S. and global hit in 1992, but the two movies could not be more different in tone. *Silence of the Lambs* plays up its two celebrities, Jodie Foster and Anthony Hopkins, and gives them a strong, caricatured presence in the movie. They engage in witty repartee and are made into glamorous figures. The last segment of the movie plays the viewer for mechanical suspense, as Jodie Foster chases down another serial killer. *Dr. Lamb* is a far scarier entry. It never plays the viewer for suspense but, instead, reveals its denouement at the beginning. The killer is a sullen and nasty figure, rather than the charismatic and articulate Anthony Hopkins playing Hannibal Lecter. We see the killer dismembering his victims, indulging his perverse fetishes, and having brutal arguments with his family. There is no feeling of resolution offered at the end; rather, the viewer is left feeling uneasy. Not surprisingly, *Dr. Lamb* has never been released in the U.S. market.

## ■ The Future of Global Cinema

It remains an open question whether Hollywood will gain or lose relative market position over the next few years. European cinema does show some encouraging signs. In the year 2000, for instance, French films captured 60 percent of their domestic market, the most in twenty years, largely because of a few hit comedies. More generally, most of the major Western European countries are relying less on subsidies to support their culture. None have cut their movie industries loose, but the long-run trend appears to lie in this direction.[36]

European governments are understandably reluctant to remove cinematic subsidies. Once the dynamic of Hollywood export superiority is in place, most European productions, as we know them, cannot survive without governmental assistance. In the short run, laissez-faire would likely lead to a greater Hollywood presence in European cinema. But in the long run, European moviemakers would be induced to make a more commercially appealing product, and not necessarily at the expense of artistic quality. The natural European advantage is in making art-house films, not blockbusters or special-effects spectaculars.

Hollywood holds a potentially vulnerable market position, given how much it spends on celebrity salaries and marketing. While these expenses give Hollywood movies a huge global boost, they also mean that American moviemakers have lost their ability to control their costs, often a sign of forthcoming commercial weakness. Witness the history of the once-dominant American auto industry. Digital technology also promises to open up moviemaking to outsiders, by lowering the costs of production.

[36] On the recent French success, see A. James (2001).

The history of cinema shows many times over that a truly great movie can be made for very small sums of money. Films of this kind may not outdraw *Titanic* at the box office, but they could resuscitate cinema in the countries where it is currently floundering. Of course it remains an open question whether European moviemakers will fill this market niche, or whether Asia has already beaten them to it.

Nonetheless it is possible for Europeans to reverse unfavorable trends, as they have in the past. In 1973, Hollywood held only 23 percent of the Italian market, and large numbers of high-quality Italian movies were commercially viable. Hollywood had dominated the Italian market after the Second World War, but Italian moviemakers fought back, in part using the techniques they learned from studying Hollywood releases.[37]

Ideally, European governments would like to return to something like the 1930–1970 period. These years show that the strong presence of Hollywood in world markets does not mean an end to European moviemaking.

After the Second World War, European movies typically did receive subsidies, but of a much smaller magnitude than today. Martin Dale estimates that in 1960 subsidies accounted for only 20 percent of the average European film, compared to his current estimate of 70 percent. The notable movies of Truffaut, Fellini, Visconti, Bergman, and others were fundamentally money-making endeavors, aimed at the competitive marketplace, despite the involvement of government at various levels.[38]

Going back earlier, the 1930s in particular were a "golden age" for French cinema; the best-known French films of this era include *L'Atalante* (Jean Vigo), *Le Jour se lève* (Marcel Carné), *La Chienne, The Grand Illusion*, and *The Rules of the Game* (all by Jean Renoir). Over thirteen hundred French feature films were issued, covering a wide range of genres. During this period, French cinema received no government subsidies. The legal restrictions on American films were in-

[37] See Muscio (2000, p. 127).
[38] See Dale (1997, p. 123).

significant and did not keep Hollywood productions out of the French market.[39]

In the early silent era, France dominated world cinema markets. Before the First World War, French movies accounted for up to seventy percent of the American market, and even more in Latin America. In a reversal of contemporary trends, American filmmakers charged the French with cultural imperialism and asked Washington for trade protection. It was commonly charged that European movies encouraged lax morals and corrupted American culture. The French responded by noting the openness of their cinematic markets and asking America to compete on equal terms. Like Hollywood today, the French market dominance was achieved without significant subsidies from the French government.[40]

Global cinema is in any case flourishing today, most of all in Asia. As for European cinema, its best hope is to rediscover an economic and cultural dynamic that combines both commercialism and creativity. Such a dynamic will require reliance on international markets and global capital, and is unlikely to flourish in a narrowly protectionist setting. The marketplace never guarantees a favorable result, but excessive insulation from competitive pressures can virtually guarantee an unfavorable result, whether economically or aesthetically.

---

[39] See Crisp (1993, p. 12), Andrew (1983, p. 57), Hayes (1930, pp. 194–95), and Sklar (1975, p. 222). Quotas limited American films to seven-eighths of the market, which was more than the American share had ever been. Gomery (1985, p. 31) argues that French quotas, which were enforced in a changing and complex manner, had some effects on American exports, but even in his account the effect is a small one, limiting Hollywood exports by no more than 15 percent.

[40] On early French dominance, see Abel (1999), Pearson (1997, p. 23), Roud (1993, p. 7), Armes (1985, pp. 19–23), and Abel (1984, p. 6; 1994). On the plea for government assistance, see Puttnam (1998, p. 41).

# 5
## ■ Dumbing Down and the Least Common Denominator

Walt Whitman remarked, "To have great poets, there must be great audiences too." It is not enough to recruit buyers, they must also be able to judge quality. High-quality audiences inspire performers, provide financial support, monitor the quality of culture, and enforce standards of competitive excellence. Their tastes embody wisdom about the quality of the product. Sir Joshua Reynolds, in his *Discourses on Art*, pronounced, "The highest ambition of every Artist is to be thought a man of Genius." To achieve such a designation, the most accomplished artists need a properly appreciative audience.[1]

French cooking is so delicious, and so successful in world markets, in part because the native French audience demands so much from its chefs. Chefs who have trained and cooked in France have passed through a culinary milieu of unparalleled rigor and competitiveness. They must cook to please a local customer base with the highest standards, and they know that their most delicious creations will meet with enthusiastic approval.

Ignorant customers damage quality just as well-informed customers support it. Many "tourist arts" are sold to transient and ill-

---

[1] See Clausen (1981, p. 129).

informed buyers. African masks are marketed en masse at tourist stands and in airport shops. Most of the buyers are looking for exotic souvenirs, and they do not spend much time discerning if the design is a generic knock-off and workmanship is slipshod. Suppliers respond by putting low quality on the market, which explains why the best and most valuable masks, according to the standards of art critics, are those made for tribal dancing rather than for tourists.

How does cross-cultural exchange affect the quality of consumer taste? Do market forces encourage suppliers to appeal to the "least common denominator" when marketing their wares to broad audiences? Why is the phrase "dumbing down" sometimes used to describe the modern era? Does product variety, as brought by a globalized culture, encourage superficial and poorly informed tastes?

These questions do not yield simple answers. As I stress throughout this book, markets bring more homogeneity *and* more diversity. This dual trend characterizes consumer taste as well as cultural products more generally. Modern taste is becoming neither uniformly more informed nor uniformly less informed.

We see cultural horrors and cultural wonders at the same time. American television talk and game shows arguably are becoming dumber, more superficial, and more sensationalistic. They are pandering to the extant level of taste. In times past, Pulitzer Prize–winning books were frequently best-sellers, today they hardly ever are.

At the same time the quality and sophistication of modern taste staggers the imagination. Growing numbers of niche consumers use the modern world to become fantastically well informed about their chosen interests. These hobbies, or sometimes life passions, run the gamut from gamelan music to African cinema to postcolonial fiction, among literally thousands of possibilities. The diverse information available in a modern book or CD superstore would not have been imaginable a century ago. The world also has more experts who know more about a greater number of cultural goods than ever before. Even small areas of global culture have their partisans who study and appreciate them with great fervor, often with the assistance of the Internet or other modern technologies.

So we should reject any simple story about dumbing down. The overall picture is one where quality taste survives and indeed flourishes in a world of cross-cultural exchange, even when many tastes appear ill informed, poorly thought out, or depraved.

## ■ Least-Common-Denominator Effects

A very simple and powerful mechanism suggests that cross-cultural exchange will make taste more informed and more diverse. As we have already seen, a general growth in the size of the market makes it possible to support many more artistic forms. Large audiences also encourage the transfer of new technologies across regions. Chapter 2 presented several examples—reggae music, Haitian art, and Persian carpets—of how foreign buyers stimulated new styles and genres in other locales. In these cases diversity rose, both within each culture and across cultures. The quality and diversity of taste rose in corresponding fashion. The new artistic forms educated many customers, and encouraged them to take an interest in cultures outside their own.

The alternative view charges that globalization encourages creative artists to pitch their products to the least common denominator. That is, the supplier may market a popular product that offers something to everyone, but at the expense of lasting product quality, as might be defined by a professional critic. Supposedly the result is a dumbing down of cultural content.[2]

Romu Sippy, a Bombay producer, tried to explain why popular Indian films so commonly choose a safe middle course: "Mythological films are not popular . . . because they offend the Muslim people.

[2] The "superstars" argument, recently popularized by Robert Frank and Philip Cook (1995), is sometimes linked to the least-common-denominator argument. It charges that product reproducibility causes all customers to flock to the favorite in the market, thus diminishing diversity. Putting Madonna on compact disc, for instance, may dry up the market for the local bar singer. I consider this argument at length in chapter 5 of my *What Price Fame?* (Cowen 2000), concluding that product reproducibility usually stimulates interest in both the highest-level and middling performers in the market. When customers do not agree on what is best, reproducibility will help creators of many different kinds make a living. In any case, the superstars argument is distinct from issues of globalization and cross-cultural exchange.

Regional films are okay, but they cannot appeal to people who do not speak the language. If you make a *dacoit* [bandit] movie, you miss out on the South, where they don't have *dacoits*. Westernized movies may be popular among the educated people of the cities, but what about the rickshaw wallah, the small vendor, the villager? If you get an Adult Certificate [equivalent to an X-rating], you miss out on the young audience. If you make a good, clean film, it may be well received by the critics, but commercially it will do nothing. Even a little sex is likely to offend the orthodox Hindu in Uttar Pradesh who goes to see a film first to find out if it is suitable for his daughters. The only thing that all people can relate to and understand is *action*."[3]

In similar fashion, Hollywood strives to present the universal to global audiences. As Hollywood markets its films to more non-English speakers, those films become more general. Action films are favored over movies with subtle dialogue. Comedy revolves around slapstick rather than verbal puns. There is relatively little that the world as a whole, or even a select group of fifty million global consumers, can agree on. So suppliers sometimes market their creations to larger groups rather than smaller ones. The relevant questions are whether any kinds of diversity suffer as a result, and whether cross-cultural exchange exacerbates or improves the negative aspects of this phenomenon.

## ■ Fixed Costs and Diversity

To understand the least-common-denominator effect, we must step back and examine the notion of "fixed costs," to use economic language. A fixed cost, by definition, is incurred regardless of how large the audience is. In that case, production requires a minimum scale to be profitable.

To provide a simple example, New York City has many live theaters, but small towns typically do not have any. The audience in a small town is not large enough to cover the fixed costs of setting up

---

[3] See Iyer (1989, pp. 248–49).

the stage, paying the cast, and so on. Any theater in a low population environment will have to draw large numbers of customers from a small base, which means marketing a product of general interest. Transvestite theater may draw hundreds in New York City or Berlin, but probably not in Topeka.

For purposes of contrast, fixed costs are low when we hire local teenagers to pick the weeds off our lawns. Not much minimum scale is needed to set the service in motion, since the weed pickers do not invest much in fixed technology. The service is economically viable even when only a few home-owners demand weed pickers. But to the extent that fixed costs rise, say a lawn mower is needed, the number of customers must increase if the service is to be supplied profitably.

Most forms of culture involve some level of fixed costs (note that I used the noncultural example of a weed picker for a case of zero fixed costs, cultural analogs are hard to find). The skills of the artist typically require a great investment in training, no matter how many customers are later served. Or in the case of movies, a certain amount of money must be spent marketing the film and setting up the theater.

Fixed costs are the bane of product diversity and limit customer choice. All other things being equal, consumer choice rises as fixed costs fall. Low fixed costs mean that markets will serve niche and minority tastes and that the menu of choice will be broad rather than narrow.

Fortunately cross-cultural exchange typically lowers fixed costs and thus renders the least common denominator effect less likely in the aggregate. The international transfer of new technologies and new ideas has been marked throughout cultural history. European literature as we know it, and the printing press, would not have come to fruition, without the introduction of paper through China and the Islamic world. Spectacles and the ink pen were no less important. Modern markets in cinema and electronically reproducible music rely on technological innovations from many countries as well. In all of these cases, trade between regions has lowered fixed costs of production and enriched the menu of choice.

Although this overall picture is strongly positive, we can imagine hypothetical examples where a larger audience leads to less product diversity. For instance, assume that only a certain number of films will be produced in a year, due to fixed costs. A larger audience might encourage filmmakers to go after mainstream taste rather than satisfying the intense preferences of smaller groups. In this case larger world markets could limit variety rather than stimulating it.

Empirically, however, we find strong evidence that large potential audiences support product diversity. Larger cities typically have more diverse cultural offerings than do much smaller cities or rural areas. Refer back to the comparison between theaters in New York City and theaters in a less populated area. The theaters in New York City are far more diverse in their offerings, largely because of higher audience demand. The greater the number of customers, the greater the ease of covering the costs of a particular production. Whether we look at music, theater, literary readings, bookstores, or other measures of cultural activity, we find greater variety in the larger cities and the wealthier economic regions.

Cinema probably provides the strongest case for the least-common-denominator effect. I will not recap the analysis of chapter 4 here, but suffice it to say that cinematic commercialism and exportation favor cinematic diversity more than is commonly believed.

The least-common-denominator effect does pop up in some other contexts. Sometimes many audience members wish to consume the same product in common. Many fans wish to watch the same Super Bowl or follow the same movie stars as do their peers, if only to have something to talk about. Individuals around the world have attached their loyalties to Madonna, Michael Jordan, and Tiger Woods, if only to feel part of some broader community. In these cases larger audiences can induce greater blandness or generality of the product, causing a least-common-denominator effect. To the extent everyone is looking to share a *common* experience in the first place, the larger audience does not necessarily stimulate more diverse outputs. A larger audience will cause suppliers to look for a commodity or experience that can be shared by the larger number of customers. This sets off a search for the least common denominator amongst the larger customer group.

But even in this case homogenization does not squeeze out diversity. Individuals do not care only about sharing a common experience with others, to the exclusion of all other values. They also seek cultural experiences that will distinguish themselves from others, or provide special and unique meaning to their lives. Larger markets help customers get what they want in these regards, by mobilizing constituencies to cover the fixed costs for as many products as possible. So when audience growth supports a least-common-denominator effect in the center of a market, it simultaneously supports more diversity at the fringes. The spread of bland "megastars" is part and parcel of the same process that brings us more "mini-stars" and more figures of cult attachment.

Finally, culture for the least common denominator is not always bad, once that concept is properly understood. To the extent that people want to share a common experience, the market delivers this opportunity. We should not seek diversity in each and every manifestation of our culture. Many people like being able to talk about the same sports teams or the same celebrities with their friends. Or sometimes they like sharing common attachments and common hobbies with strangers in distant countries. Least common denominator culture is most plausibly bad when the main offering is the *only* offering and markets are unable to support diversity and niche attachments at the fringes. As we have already seen, this is most certainly not true of the modern world.

The phrase "least common denominator" is emotionally charged to sound undesirable. The words "least" and "common" have negative connotations, while "denominator" sounds cold, like a kind of commercial mathematics that would be inimical to creative culture. No person, especially no intellectual elitist, would be inclined to support a culture with this description. On closer examination, however, the underlying concept resembles the notion of "universality," a word with more positive connotations. A universal cultural product deals with general features of the human condition and appeals to a wide number and diversity of human beings. Is this not part of what the world is supposed to provide?

## ■ How We Consume, and the Quality of Taste

Another version of the least-common-denominator argument suggests that larger markets will be populated by less intelligent or less sophisticated customers. Perhaps the new customers entering the market are less able than the previous customers, or perhaps the quality of taste declines more generally as markets grow. Logically speaking, this worry is more plausible than the least-common-denominator argument taken alone. The least-common-denominator effect, even when it operates, is a problem only if the new denominator of market taste is low or degraded by some standard.

To see whether cross-cultural exchange and product variety are likely to damage the quality of customer taste, let us proceed with some definitions. I call consumption *intensive* to the extent that a consumer concentrates time, energy, and attention on the goods in question. Alternatively, consumption is *extensive* to the extent that consumers scatter their attention, rather than focusing it. We are intensive consumers when we read every available Beethoven biography, buy multiple performances of each symphony on compact disc, and refer to the musical score while listening. This behavior helps support the higher-quality Beethoven products, rather than the lower-quality ones.[4]

We are extensive consumers when we channel-surf with a remote-control switcher, and move rapidly from one program to the next. I use the term "channel surfers" to refer to this kind of consumer more generically. A channel surfer will move quickly from one Web page to another, pick up ten novels but finish none of them, or buy many compact discs but never listen carefully to any of them.

Whether an individual consumes intensively or extensively often depends on context. If I were moving to a foreign country, and

---

[4] I am indebted to Andy Rutten for the "extensive" and "intensive" terminology.

could take only a few English-language books along, I might bring Shakespeare and Spenser, two classic authors who merit multiple careful readings, to keep myself busy for many nights. When I live next door to a free public library with a large selection, I am more likely to bring home a handful of browsable works that may or may not pay off in terms of quality. If my selections are disappointing, I can return to the library for more. When I have the entire Web at my disposal, I rarely spend much time with a single site or page.

In part, we are intensive or extensive consumers by our emotional or intellectual natures, or because we follow the lead of our social peers. But in part our mode of consuming is shaped by our opportunities, including the extent of cross-cultural trade.[5]

The notion of a "throw-away culture" represents the European caricature of the United States, or of commercialism more generally. In this vision, a cornucopia of products leads individuals to casually sample goods before disposing of them and moving on to the next one. In more analytic terms, opportunities rise more rapidly than the amount of time and attention available for consumption. No technological development gives us more than twenty-four hours in a day. Rising leisure time, higher life expectancy, and greater shopping ease all expand the time for cultural consumption, but not enough to keep pace with the growth in products.[6]

According to this argument, if *everyone* is "just passing through" in their consumption activity, audience attention will be spread very thinly. Audience members will not judge quality accu-

---

[5] The movement from 78-rpm records to LPs to compact discs has made some kinds of music consumption less intensive. The inconveniences of 78s were in part a blessing in disguise. The clumsiness of the technology and the short length of the side (approximately three minutes) made it difficult for the listener to do anything other than listen to the music. This technology encouraged careful listening, and thus it encouraged music that stood up to careful listening. Today many listeners put on a seventy-nine-minute CD at high volume and walk around cleaning the house, which encourages a more casual kind of listening, and thus a more casual kind of music.

[6] Staffan Linder (1970) wrote of the "increasingly harried" leisure class. Linder noted that while economic growth increases the number of commodities in the market, the amount of time in a day is fixed. Linder viewed the consumer of leisure as fundamentally harried, having far more activities available than he or she could ever exploit. His vision of the market economy is one of high blood pressure, traffic jams,

rately when they consume, or insist on quality from the producers. Creators, in turn, might respond by offering homogeneous pap, produced at low cost and failing to meet exacting standards of originality. Product variety thus runs the risk of being the Faustian bargain of modern culture. We can sample many more products, but this freedom implies that many consumers will put less time and effort into each one.

It is not hard to find examples of this mechanism. Tourists, for instance, tend to be extensive rather than intensive consumers. Often they choose restaurants randomly, or because other tourists have recommended them. It costs them too much time and effort to find out which places are the best. At the highest end of the price scale, tourists consult the reliable Michelin guide and travel far for a special meal. But for most segments of the market, the food lover should look for a restaurant frequented by the locals, who know the best places. When we see a dining room full of tourists, the meal is probably generic rather than original.

In a world of fully globalized culture, both customers and goods would be extremely mobile. The fear is that all cultural relationships would, in essence, be tourist relationships. A culture of this kind might be fast and convenient, like a fast-food restaurant in a train station, but lacking in originality, creativity, or sustained attention to excellence and innovative detail. Critics of globalization do not typically refer to formal models for their arguments. But in effect their "dumbing-down" claim suggests that cross-cultural exchange favors extensive consumption at the expense of intensive consumption. The fear is that everyone becomes a careless "cultural tourist," and randomly samples a wide variety of global commodities, with little attention to the quality of any one of them.

This fear has more substance than the elitist criticism that market-driven culture serves the masses rather than meeting a higher calling. Even if we use the economist's standard of satisfying con-

---

and the Christmas shopping rush, all because of economic growth. In contrast to Staffer's concern for psychological pressures, I focus on how diversity affects individual decisions to monitor product quality.

sumer preferences, markets may provide more mediocrity and superficiality than consumers—meaning non-elitist consumers—ideally would like.

The production of quality culture involves a collective action dilemma amongst consumers. Individual consumers, for instance, may choose too much channel-surfing from a collective point of view. Each individual will maximize his or her gain, not taking the aggregate effect of their activities—a kind of cultural cheapening—into account. Too many products will end up as mediocre, as consumers will not choose a socially ideal mix of intensive and extensive consumption.

Using similar logic, customers tend to underinvest in the refinement of their tastes. We can think of taste refinement as one means of monitoring product quality. When all fans in a market invest in improving their tastes, creators are forced to meet higher standards, to the benefit of all consumers. Yet in a broad market no fan, acting on his or her own, would gain much from a personal investment in taste improvement. If I improve my taste in food, the local Chinese restaurant does not respond with a better product. The chef does not care what I think, given that I comprise a very small part of his market. In addition to the time and energy I would have invested, I may simply end up frustrated by my new and higher standards for food. Yet if we could *all* improve our taste in Chinese food, and learn to discern the better product, the chef would be compelled to upgrade his offerings, to the benefit of consumers more generally.[7]

On a global scale, the entire world benefits from the fact that French diners have good taste. Successful creators typically refine

---

[7] The market failure argument requires that the consumers prefer the superior product, once it is presented to them. Even customers with "low-quality tastes" distinguish between higher- and lower-quality versions of what they like. They would, for instance, prefer to view a superior soap opera, rather than an inferior soap opera, even if they would not wish to replace the soap opera with Rembrandt or Proust. For this reason the argument is not paternalistic. The possibility of market failure also requires some assumptions about the supply side of the market. The creator will have market power and thus can offer an extra increment of quality, if induced to do so, at a market value above its marginal cost of production. If taste refinement in-

their initial skills to satisfy a demanding local customer base, only later shipping those skills out to other markets. If the citizens of Paris and Lyon suddenly lost their interest in food, the outlook for fine dining would be bleaker, not just in France but across the world. The French market in top-rate chefs provides high standards and a training milieu which benefit many people—customers and chefs alike—who have paid little or nothing for the basic infrastructure.

## ■ The Resilience of Informed Consumption

The above logic does provide an account of some observed homogenizing and dumbing-down trends. Fortunately, cultural consumption has not become more superficial across the board. The rise of channel surfers is only one part of a broader trend of increasing *diversity* of consumption methods. High-quality taste, and high-quality customer monitoring, have shown a great resilience and in many regards have flourished without precedent.

Extensive and intensive consumption tend to rise and fall together, just as homogenization and heterogenization tend to move in tandem. Additional "bad taste" is one by-product of larger markets and the diversity those markets generate.

Product variety encourages intensive monitoring as well as channel-surfing. Tastes are diverse and many individuals would like to specialize their consumption, rather than channel-surf, but only if they can find something they really enjoy. As the variety of products rises, more of these (diverse) individuals can find pursuits to fascinate them. If meat and potatoes dominate the food market, I will not monitor either intensively; if I can buy spicy Asian curries, my monitoring interests will take on a more fanatical and more concentrated slant. The members of the Japanese "mola club" are fascinated with the textiles from the San Blas Islands off the coast of Panama, hardly a mainstream preoccupation. They study these textiles, trade them, and have visited the world's largest mola gallery in Santa Fe.

---

duces more quality, that increase is welfare-improving in terms of economic efficiency, in addition to improving the quality of culture.

Were it not for the global presence of molas, many of these individuals would engage in cultural monitoring less fervently. The molas stimulate their interest and draw forth their monitoring efforts.

I call individuals of this slant *hobbyists*. Hobbyists wish to specialize their cultural consumption, and engage in intense monitoring, *if* they can find the right opportunities. Cross-cultural exchange has proved a boon to hobbyists and hobbyist monitoring. The greater menu of candidate commodities, and greater publicity for those commodities, improves the chance that would-be hobbyists find a good match.

Hobbyists and channel surfers complement each other symbiotically. Just as the channel surfers rely on the hobbyists to monitor quality, so do the hobbyists rely on the channel surfers. Channel surfers create external benefits for other consumers, just as intensive monitors do. By sampling a wide variety of commodities, even if they do so indiscriminately, channel surfers help finance variety. The resulting increase in variety supports diverse and appealing monitoring opportunities for the hobbyists. A creative environment thus balances intensive and extensive consumption, rather than favoring the former exclusively.

The most sophisticated consumers combine intensive and extensive consumption. Many hobbyists appreciate their specialties, and judge quality accurately, only because they have been exposed to a wide variety of other products. A listener who had heard only Mozart might not understand the composer very well. The individual who repeatedly watches the same soap-opera episode on videotape is an intensive consumer, but not necessarily to the benefit of anyone else.

Customers must refer to standards if they are to accurately judge the quality of local products. These standards are inevitably comparative in nature and therefore require exposure to other cultures. American customers who have sampled European food typically have higher standards for fresh ingredients and good bread than those who have not. European customers have demanded better salad bars from their restaurants, following visits to the United States. French Impressionist paintings, by stimulating the imagination of buyers, have spurred native schools of painting around the world. America, in the early part of the twentieth century, brought in French masterworks for the famous Armory Show of 1913. These artworks not only inspired and taught American painters, but they also stimulated the demands of American buyers and created a base of avid collectors for modern art.

Channel surfers and intensive consumers benefit from the same consumption technologies. Remote control switchers, for instance, enable hobbyists to find new programs—possibly to become their favorite ones—more easily than before. The jet airplane allows wealthy American sophisticates to monitor Parisian restaurants with relative frequency. Musical recording, by enabling repeated listenings of the same work, makes it easier to study many kinds of music. Many fans use VCRs to concentrate their viewing—they watch *Star Trek*, *The Simpsons*, or *Seinfeld* several times a week rather than just once, and they develop a deeper understanding of the show. The art museum, largely a modern phenomenon, allows viewers to see the same paintings and sculptures many times over and thus helps refine their taste in art. The Internet can support intensive study of a given area, not just the broad and rapid sampling of many Web sites.

Channel-surfing technologies bring fans together and allow them to act as a coordinated unit. Science fiction novels, for instance, have avid and well-informed readers. These fans devote time and care to monitoring the quality of what they read, organizing fan clubs and conventions, publicizing the better works, and so on. They use the Internet, or relatively cheap travel opportunities, to stay in touch with each other. These individuals act as a local customer base in the relevant sense, by monitoring and enforcing quality, even though their residences are spread through a wide geographic area. Unlike in the past, the idea of a "local" customer base is no longer defined or limited by geography.

115

Note that hobbyists enable a globalized culture to retain many of the advantages of narrower and more specialized cultures. Even if hobbyists are relatively small in number, their fervent interest and involvement help them enforce quality and originality in the cultural goods they follow. The quality of consumer monitoring depends on (at least) two factors: how many consumers are monitoring each good, and how much effort and expertise each consumer puts into monitoring that good. Even if product variety leads to fewer monitors per good, the monitors that remain are likely to be fervent and well informed, which will support quality standards.

The global nature of a market may, by itself, encourage fervent customer-monitoring. Through the mechanism of *pride*, the international success of French food has prompted many French to take an interest in their cuisine. Rising young French chefs remain subject to immediate and intense local scrutiny, thereby improving both French and global cuisine. Jamaicans identify with reggae music in similar fashion, in large part because of its global success. Reggae was originally a minority taste in Jamaica, identified with the rebellious young, but now it is regarded as a national treasure.

The expressive delight of changing the world, or spreading one's tastes to others, encourages many individuals to monitor the quality of cultural outputs. Fan-created Web pages, many of which track or monitor cultural creators, have proliferated, even though few of these authors reap material rewards for their efforts. Rather, the Web-page creators enjoy expressing their opinions and reaching others. The Internet encourages individuals to become well-informed experts in cultural fields, so that they may communicate their opinions to broader audiences. In other words, individuals do not monitor simply to improve the quality of their consumption. Many consumers enjoy the monitoring process as a source of expressive pleasure or as a means of communicating their tastes to others.

Zagat's food guides rely on the recommendations and reports of their local readers, and then communicate this information to a broader clientele, including tourists and visitors. The popularity and reach of Zagat's has made readers more willing to send in recommendations, rather than less willing. Zagat's has increased the strength of the local customer bases in the areas it surveys, by putting local customers in touch with each other and by motivating their reporting efforts. In a typical year, over one hundred thousand individuals contribute to the Zagat's ratings and the number is growing. Many individuals, including this author, self-publish their own evaluations on their personal Web pages; my own ethnic dining guide for the Washington D.C. area is thirty-five pages long.[8]

Many sources of intensive consumption will remain robust in a diverse and globalized economy. Many consumers resist variety or consciously organize themselves to preserve a culture they identify with. These individuals contribute to local culture out of fierce loyalties, traditions, habits, or perhaps even prejudices. Some of these local customer bases are based on a degree of provincialism and a distrust of the cosmopolitan.

Minority groups, outsiders, and victims of discrimination are more likely to consume intensively, even in wealthy and relatively open societies. These individuals feel shut out by the orientation of many mainstream cultural products, and they specialize their consumption accordingly. Institutions and norms within these minority communities strengthen such tendencies, as the "local" cultural goods become identifiers of status within the community. African-Americans, for instance, devote a disproportionate share of their attention to African-American cultural products, which helps maintain intensive monitoring in these genres.[9]

Most young consumers engage in intensive consumption to an almost fanatical degree. Few of today's young are looking for a comprehensive knowledge of world culture, but, rather, they seek to master the same relatively small number of cultural products that command the attention of their peers. Teenagers are not cultural omnivores. They go see the same movie many times in a row or listen to the same album repeatedly.

[8] On Zagat's, see Harmon (1998).
[9] An alternative and complementary explanation for the cultural vitality of some minorities, such as African-Americans, focuses on the greater propensity of such art-

Youth thus provides a permanent base of intensive consumption in a market economy. Individuals between twelve and twenty years old, while they account for 15 percent of the American population, make up 30 percent of the movie audience. Individuals twenty-four and under make up 40 percent of the movie audience. For the categories of rock, pop, black/urban, and country, 40 percent of all purchases were bought by consumers under the age of twenty-four. Adolescent purchasing power has been rising for many decades and probably will continue to do so. According to one estimate, in 1990 fifteen- to seventeen-year-olds spent $23 billion of their own money and influenced $90 billion of their parents' spending.[10]

Even if we believe that today's youth supports a good deal of low-quality junk, the young also provide the monitoring behind some real cultural excellence. Many of the notable contemporary revolutions in music have come from youth cultures and audiences, including the Beatles and the Rolling Stones, Motown, rap music, and Seattle Grunge. Each of these styles later found favor with many older listeners, but it was the young who served as the original monitors of innovation and quality.

The intensive consumption of the young does, if nothing else, force producers to meet standards of a certain sort. In television, both *Star Trek* (the original series) and *The Simpsons* started with a very young audience but later achieved a more general canonical status. The *Star Wars* movie was originally aimed at young audiences, and its creators included features that would make the movie suitable for repeated viewings, such as a history and a background for the relevant characters. This mythology has subsequently become a significant feature of movie culture more generally, and not just for the young.

Finally, professional critics act as specialized monitors in support of quality and diversity. Customers pay experts and critics for advice and specialized knowledge, whether explicitly through fees

---

ists to take risks, given that they have little to lose in terms of establishment connections and have fewer mainstream job opportunities.

[10] See Stipp (1993), and Christenson and Roberts (1998, pp. 15–16).

or implicitly through viewing advertising. Critics represent a division of labor, allowing markets to economize on how much monitoring is needed.

We normally think of hotel restaurants as having relatively low quality and high prices, given that they have a more or less captive audience of hotel guests. Other restaurants may be far away or the guests have greater trust in the establishment that is putting them up. Either way, hotel restaurants are a potential recipe for mediocrity.

At the highest levels of excellence, however, we find many restaurants in hotels, as a quick perusal of the Michelin dining guides will confirm. For meals costing $100 and up, the price is too high to rely on a regular clientele of locals alone. Instead, such restaurants draw on wealthy and sophisticated tourists and traveling gourmets, in addition to the local wealthy. In effect these individuals commission critics—usually Michelin or Gault-Milleau reviewers—to tell them which restaurants deserve their patronage.

Critics, of course, do not remedy all quality problems. Many customers refrain from paying for critics, preferring instead to free ride on the efforts and expenditures of others. They hope to hear a critic's opinion from other customers, or they try to infer critical opinion by observing which products are popular. For this reason, it can be difficult for a critic to make a good living. Furthermore, customers who cannot judge the quality of a product may be equally unable to judge the quality of a critic. Critics may only push back the problem to another level. For the same reason that levels of taste are too low, each consumer may underinvest in monitoring the quality of the critic.

Critics and experts tend to be most effective when the evaluated item is large in value, relative to the effort required to assess it. Experts are hired to assess the quality of diamonds, but not the quality of brass. We buy *Consumer Reports* to evaluate new cars or stereos on the market, but not new brands of thumbtacks or paper clips. Similarly, it is easier to find reliable dining guides for top restaurants than for local diners. The critic, who faces some fixed cost for producing evaluations, finds it most profitable to evaluate high-value cultural products, such as fancy meals or expensive paintings. When an art collector is considering a bid on a van Gogh painting, he or she will consult a critic about the painting's authenticity.

For these reasons, the wealthy face the least danger of quality erosion in a globalized culture. Most individuals who purchase expensive products—diamonds, original paintings, and "Michelin restaurant" meals—are well-to-do and will consult or hire critics. Even if cross-cultural exchange lowers product quality in some areas, due to the weakening of customer monitoring, the wealthy will remain protected. Poorer individuals eat more frequently in local diners and more generally consume items that are small in value. They rely on fellow customers to monitor quality, rather than on professional critics, and therefore face a greater danger of the collective action problems discussed above.[11]

## ■ Brand Names

The recent "No Logo" movement has rebelled against capitalist brands as forces for cultural homogenization. Across the United States, individuals are proclaiming their "liberation" from consuming brand name goods, in the hope of making society more beautiful and more diverse.[12]

To see why individuals might find brands objectionable, let us step back for a moment and see what brands do. Typically markets use brand names to ensure product quality. When consumers do not have the time or energy to investigate the merits of a particular product, they rely on the brand name as an informational shorthand. We have a reasonable idea what to expect when we walk into a Nordstrom outlet, a McDonald's store, or a Wolfgang Puck restau-

---

[11] Of course, not all the individuals who buy paintings and Michelin-restaurant meals are relatively wealthy. Some of these consumers simply place great value on culture and dining, and spend their money accordingly. Similarly, not everyone who goes to the diner is poor; some of the wealthy do not care or bother to buy expensive food, for whatever reasons. In these cases, the benefits of globalization follow the love of expensive art, not the wealth. The relatively poor buyer of paintings still will benefit from global culture, whereas the rich man who goes to diners will not.

[12] On the No Logo movement, see the recent book by Naomi Klein (2000).

rant. The operating authority of the New Jersey Turnpike, in its wisdom, installed nationally known fast-food chains at its rest stops, to improve dining quality. Drivers who visit Turnpike rest stops now know exactly what they will get.

These informational functions of brands, despite their practical benefits, can shift the balance towards standardized products and away from the unique or the creative. Generating a nationally known brand name often requires a homogeneous product on a national or regional scale. Franchisees who deviate from the basic formula are terminated or sued.

Barbecue food, which is rarely found in national chains, provides a useful contrast. It has a stronger regional component (North Carolina barbecue differs greatly from Texas barbecue), the production technology involves barbecue pits and sauces that are difficult to replicate, and the clientele is built around local audiences with strong tastes for particular food styles. Barbecue remains a local tradition and for the most part has not been successfully franchised on a national or international scale.

Much of contemporary American food, with its Jell-O, Cheetos, frozen TV dinners, and Big Macs, represents a nightmare come true for critics of commercial society. National marketing of a brand requires many different producers or franchisees to replicate the basic product. But replicability limits complexity and innovation. The nature of quality must be articulable, and the parent company must be able to monitor that quality with relative ease; in other words, brand-name quality requires some corporate central planning. For this reason, brand-name products often are produced and marketed according to well-defined formulae.

The foodstuffs found in most American supermarkets are dominated by Borden, General Foods, Beatrice Foods, General Mills, Kellogg, Kraft, Standard Brands, Nestlé, Heinz, Pillsbury, and Campbell, among others. The large food producers and processors manufacture on a very large scale, use their size to extract price concessions when buying inputs, run a nationwide network of warehouses, and most importantly, market on a national scale. Often the dominant position goes to the firm best able to identify its corporate name with the basic product; to many Americans the brand name "Campbell" is virtually synonymous with soup. These national brands, whatever their economic efficiencies, lead to homogenization, product uniformity, and relatively bland and cheap tastes.[13]

While these points are well taken, the critics of brands overstate their case. Brands bring innovation as well as homogenization. The homogenizing trends we observe are part of a larger story about growing market-size, which brings more choice and more diversity.

Brands appear to be homogenizing ex post, once they are established in the market, but at the time of their introduction they typically are innovations. McDonald's succeeded because it was an advance over the local diner food found in many parts of America. Its french fries remain the best in many towns. Taco Bell increases choice and food diversity in many of the communities it enters, even if it does not count as true Mexican food. It also has paved the way for many individuals to try other, more innovative Mexican food products.

Morton's steak chain, which has several dozen branches, provides high-quality meats, distributed from central warehouses in the Chicago area and marketed under a restaurant brand name. Homogeneity results in the sense that each Morton's is similar. Yet dining in each community becomes more diverse: northern Virginia, the home of the Morton's closest to this author, now has high-quality beef from the Midwest.

American supermarkets are full of national brands, but at the same time they carry more exotic and high-quality foods then be-

---

[13] See Levenstein (1993). We observe the homogenizing effect of brand names in many contexts, not just cuisine. Manhattan, for instance, is becoming the province of tourists. Major Manhattan avenues, such as Fifth Avenue, are now advertising thoroughfares aimed at large audiences, especially out-of-towners. Major national and international chains purchase prominent space in New York for purposes of advertising. The stores are not always expected to make money, as long as they publicize the brand name to enough visitors. The geographic space of Manhattan is becoming a billboard to increasing degree, rather than an incubator of cultural vitality. The question is not whether these practices involve some efficiency (clearly they do), but whether aesthetics and economics are working together or against each other.

fore. A variety of European-inspired commodities, from mineral water to high-quality cheese and bread, are increasingly available in the United States, in large part because consumers are demanding them. Gourmet supermarkets are spreading across cities and suburbs. These developments have been driven by the same increase in market size that led to homogeneous national brands. Furthermore, the supermarkets themselves use their brand names ("Fresh Fields" in my area) to certify the quality and freshness of nonbranded goods, thus strengthening the markets for high-quality foodstuffs.

Often a brand name certifies creativity rather than uniformity or homogeneity. The brand name may be the moniker of a highly creative individual, such as when a top chef attaches his or her name to a restaurant, or when a designer attaches his or her name to a line of clothing. The name of an artist or musician serves as a brand. If a painting is signed by Picasso or Matisse, the customer expects a certain level of quality and creativity. We do not usually think of such practices as brand names, but in fact they use the same logic, only they support diversity and high quality rather than homogenization.

Brand names allow artists to experiment with different styles, without fear of losing their "in" with the audience. Picasso changed styles many times, but his buyers knew they were getting a Picasso. If we imagine a world where artworks are produced under true anonymity (i.e., with no brands), it is not obvious that quality and diversity would improve. The most successful artists, for instance, might try to re-create their greatest triumphs, so that the audience could identify the product as theirs. Brand names remove this fear of anonymity, by telling audiences when they should take a second look or when they should pay heed to a new style.

Las Vegas receives 30 million visitors in a single year. We might expect food in Las Vegas to be very bad, but in fact it is very good. Las Vegas has arguably the highest concentration of high-quality restaurants of any city in the United States, with the possible exception of New York City. In addition to the excellent (and subsidized) food at the casinos, many of the top American restaurants, such as Emeril's (based in New Orleans) and Spago's (based in Beverly

Hills), have opened up branches in Las Vegas. The already established brand names of these restaurants certify their quality to Las Vegas tourists. The restaurants rely on the publicity generated by the home branch, which has been extensively tested and refined by a local customer base. Markets tend to economize on the number of local customer bases needed to generate high-quality products.[14]

Wolfgang Puck now has restaurants in several American cities, including one in O'Hare Airport in Chicago, and for a while had one in Mexico City. In part, these restaurants are selling the celebrity of the chef through a brand name. Whatever we may think of this dumbing down to a celebrity-hungry audience, the process supports excellent cooking. Often the chef invests only a small amount of time and effort in running the restaurant, but plays a role comparable to a "celebrity endorser." The chef puts his reputation on the line by attaching his name to the restaurant and telling potential patrons that the food is good. Branches of this sort tend to be innovative, independent establishments in their own right, even if their link to the food style of the endorsing chef is a marginal one.

Brand names, by enabling the lucrative practice of *branching*, raise the initial rewards for creativity. Creators know that they will become rich if they succeed in proving their creativity in their local environment. Nordstrom expanded to a national scale after proving itself in its original home market of the Pacific Northwest. The store has lost some of its special flavor over time, and in that sense its history reflects the homogenizing properties of brand names. Nonetheless the prospect of profitable branching helps drive innovation in the first place, even if the pathbreakers eventually merge into the mainstream of the market.

## ■ The Split of High and Low Culture

To sum up where we have arrived, there is no reason to expect that cross-cultural exchange lowers the quality of customer taste, all things considered. It is possible to identify some negative trends,

[14] On the number of visitors, see McDowell (1998).

but these developments are best understood in terms of a larger picture of diversity, innovation, and market extension. In addition, intensive hobbyist-monitoring has become more widespread, more effective, and more focused, even if it does not dominate the life of every individual.

Tocqueville, when criticizing the level of taste in democratic, commercial societies, used the historical aristocracy as his foil. We can now recast this comparison in different terms. Aristocracies concentrate buying power in the hands of a few, and thus to some extent limit the free-rider problem behind taste refinement, as discussed above. An aristocrat, patronizing art as a single buyer, or as one of a few buyers, finds that refinement of his or her taste pushes the artist to improve as well. The patron will receive better paintings if she asks that artists meet the higher standard. The incentive to refine one's taste is thus relatively high, all other things being equal.[15]

Aristocracy, however, fails to cultivate quality taste in numerous other regards. Product variety tends to be weak, and the size of the market is small. Aristocracy does not support artistic freedom, due to the relative paucity of buyers, the relative weakness of the market, and the near-exclusive identification of buyers with elite points of view. Aristocratic patrons also have limited canons of taste, in part because they have not been exposed to many ideas and styles; that is, their consumption is not sufficiently extensive. Even when the median quality of aristocratic monitoring was high, monitoring was not widespread across many markets, and it failed to draw on many different kinds of knowledge. In short, aristocracy did not provide for much diversity of taste.[16]

---

[15] Tocqueville (1969 [1835], p. 466) wrote: "Craftsmen in aristocratic societies work for a strictly limited number of customers who are very hard to please. Perfect workmanship gives the best hope of profit." See also p. 611: "In aristocracies every man has but one sole aim which he constantly pursues; but man in democracies has a more complicated existence; it is the exception if one's mind is not concerned with several aims at the same time, and these aims are often very diverse. Unable to be an expert in all, a man easily becomes satisfied with half-baked notions."

[16] Notice that cross-cultural exchange, by breaking down traditional status relationships, helps spread intensive monitoring to more commodities. Pierre Bourdieu (1986), among other commentators, stresses how the desire for distinction drives cul-

The aristocratic influence on culture declined as purchasing power spread to a broader population. New and popular cultural forms arose, making extensive consumption an option for many individuals. Many strands of mainstream culture have become more accessible and in some regards more superficial, to appeal to the channel surfers. These consumers sought cultural outputs in short, easy-to-consume bits. At the same time, hobbyists have been able to fund less-accessible products outside of mainstream channels.

In this setting high culture has become one form of hobbyist culture (although by no means the only form). It has lost its cultural centrality, but in return has gained access to numerous technologies of diversity. Classical music, for instance, now draws upon compact discs, the Penguin record guide, Internet music files, and easy transportation to the concert halls of Europe and the United States. These institutions give consumers a better selection of high-quality classical music than ever before.

We can now see one account of how high and popular culture split. In contemporary America the channel surfers consume more superficially and tend to look at the more popular items. The cultural producers who serve hobbyist demand offer intense and sophisticated products, which are admired by relatively small circles of critics, cognoscenti, and fellow creators. Professional critics, who tend to be well informed, will take the side of hobbyist culture, whose merits they are well equipped to understand. What is popular therefore diverges from what is critically acclaimed.[17]

Culture appears to be declining in quality, even when it is flourishing and becoming more diverse. The most visible and most popu-

---

tural consumption. Cultural exchange brings this mechanism into the service of diversity. In static forms of aristocracy, to provide a contrast, a relatively small number of commodities serve as indicators of social status, and these commodities receive careful attention from elites. International trade breaks down this pattern, either by making new cultural goods available to wider numbers of people, or by diverting the attention of the elites to new items. Social regroupings will occur, and competition for status will be shaken up. The number and kind of available distinctions will increase, which will create interest in new and more diverse sets of commodities.

[17] I define high culture as the products that win the strongest critical acclaim, whereas low culture consists of the most popular set of products. For more on this distinction, and the vast literature on the topic, see Cowen (1998).

lar cultural media tend to appeal to less-informed levels of customer taste, and thus make the culture look worse than it actually is.

Hobbyist favorites, virtually by definition, are culturally peripheral rather than part of the mainstream. They have a hard time achieving central status or defining a cultural era. For this reason, many of the best cultural products in a globalized world—those consumed by the hobbyists—remain hidden from most customers and from most critics as well. The proliferating hobbyist cultures are harder for outsiders to observe and appreciate, no matter how healthy and vital they may be.

We find also that external commentators are least likely to agree about hobbyist culture. Hobbyist creations, no matter how high their quality in objective aesthetic terms, will not appeal to many individuals outside the relevant set of fans. The serialist music of Pierre Boulez provides great joy to its small audience (myself included), but most people dismiss or ignore it, or perhaps hate it. *As hobbyist cultures grow, more cultural quality will come in areas that people disagree about, or simply do not know about, rather than in areas where they agree.* The quality of taste therefore will tend to appear worse than it truly is.

The fundamental story about consumer taste, in modern times, is not one of dumbing down or of producers seeking to satisfy a homogeneous least common denominator at the expense of quality. Rather, the basic trend is of increasing variety and diversity, at all levels of quality, high and low.

# 6
■■■ Should National Culture Matter?

Germany and France are more alike today than they were one hundred years ago. In part the nations have traded with each other, and in part they have shared common technological advances through other trading partners. Their convergence would accelerate if they shared political governance, as a stronger European Union would bring. In this regard, the homogenizing properties of cross-cultural exchange are evident.

This reality, however, does not demonstrate that trade fails culture. These same developments have brought more human freedom and more diversity *within* each society. The *individuals* in either French or German society have more opportunities than before and pursue more diverse cultural paths. A quick look at a modern music, video, or book store confirms the growing cornucopia of products at our disposal. Only in a world of globalized culture can I collect nineteenth-century Japanese prints, listen to the music of Pygmy tribes, read the Trinidadian author V. S. Naipaul, and enjoy the humor of Canadian Jim Carrey, while my neighbors pursue different paths of their own choosing.

The observed increases in homogeneity and heterogeneity are two sides of the same coin, rather than opposing processes. Trade, even when it supports choice and diverse achievement, homogenizes culture in the following sense: it gives individuals, regardless of their country, a similarly rich set of consumption opportunities. It makes countries or societies "commonly diverse," as opposed to making them different from each other.

This co-movement of homogenization and heterogenization is clearest in the long run. Since the beginning of humankind, the world has developed an enormous variety of musics and arts. The scope of market exchange—on the rise throughout much of this period—has supported rather than thwarted these increasingly diverse creative achievements.

At the same time individuals now share more common cultural components than before. I know many of the same songs, movies, and corporate logos as do numerous people in Bangkok. This was not true in the nineteenth century, or even as recently as thirty years ago. Different cultures have more common components than before, and individuals around the world are selecting from a commonly diverse menu of choice. The freedom to be different also means the freedom to sometimes choose the same things.

Cross-cultural trade does not eliminate difference altogether, but, rather, it liberates difference from the constraints of place. Emile Durkheim, in his nineteenth-century work on the division of labor, wrote: "Certainly different societies tend to resemble each other more, but that is not the same as saying that the individuals who compose them do so. . . . There are no longer as many differences as there are great regions, but there are almost as many as there are individuals." Ironically, individuals become more diverse only when their societies become more alike.[1]

The common argument that globalization destroys diversity assumes a collectivist concept of diversity. This metric compares one

[1] See Durkheim (1964 [1893], p. 136).

society to another, or one country to another, instead of comparing one individual to another. It also assumes that diversity takes the form of cultural differentiation across geographic space, and that this differentiation should be visible to the naked eye, such as when we cross the border between the United States and Mexico. By comparing the collectives and the aggregates, and by emphasizing geographic space, this standard begs the question as to which kind of diversity matters.

## ■ Should We Worry about National Culture?

One option is to stake out a purely individualistic position on the meaning and desirability of diversity. In this view, diversity within society—which reflects positive freedom of choice—is the relevant standard for judging cross-cultural trade. We need not worry if societies "look more alike," provided that they resemble each other by offering individuals many diverse options.

The individualist position suggests that diversity *across* societies matters only in instrumental terms. Societal differences can help expand the menu of choice, given the "paradox of diversity" discussed in chapter 3. If each society were exactly alike, we might all end up with less to choose from. Some degree of cultural specialization and difference, by generating more innovations, enriches the menu for everyone.

Diversity across societies may be useful for yet another instrumental reason. If we have no final and set vision of "the good life," the best discovery-procedure may involve competition across many distinct approaches to culture. In this regard diversity across cultures may provide purer forms of comparison and experimentation than will diversity within a culture. Within a culture it often proves hard for an individual to break from the given mold. A more insular world, if it keeps regions less alike, may provide a richer and more informative learning process.

These remarks help account for the common intuition that diversity across societies is desirable to some extent, yet without elevating that "collectivist" metric into an independent or intrinsic value. Diversity across societies, as a collectivist concept, may in fact be needed to realize a highly individualistic vision of freedom of choice across a broad range of opportunities.

Looking at polar or extreme cases appears to confirm the view that diversity across societies has primarily instrumental value, rather than intrinsic value. Imagine a world of many separate cultures, each of which specializes in the production of one cultural artifact. Each culture is homogeneous from within, even though each differs from the other greatly. This kind of diversity is worth little or nothing. Each individual faces a monolithic culture and has no positive freedom of choice. Alternatively, imagine that each society is incredibly diverse, but in similar ways. In this hypothetical world, we can go anywhere and see Javanese puppet theater, look at French Impressionist pictures, eat sushi, and hear Afro-Cuban music, all of high quality. In this attractive scenario, diversity across societies is very low, but diversity within any society is very high. Such a comparison suggests (but does not prove) that diversity within society has priority over diversity across societies, and that the latter is primarily an instrumental value.

The case for treating diversity across societies as a purely instrumental value is less strong, however, once we leave the polar cases. If the degree of choice is fairly high to begin with, additional societal or cultural distinctiveness may be more important (at the relevant margin) than having a broader menu of choice.

Many individuals value cultural difference for its own sake. Canadians wish to differ from the United States, just as many Québécois value being different from the residents of Ontario. Many individuals in each group appear willing to tolerate a less extensive menu of choice, if in return they can maintain their special status to greater degree. It is identity they seek, not choice per se. It may offend the libertarian and the cosmopolitanite to hear this, but in most cases the relevant cultural identity requires *not* having a choice about everything. This limitation upon choice is an essential feature of many cultures, even though it is not always well-advertised as such.

Even if we reject the collectivist concept of diversity across cultures as an end in itself, cultural markets work well only if individuals place intrinsic value on cultural distinctiveness. When two groups trade with each other, the members of each group use the ideas and technologies of the other to support their own notions of cultural identity, as discussed throughout this book. Trade brings diversity, rather than sameness, through identity-driven processes of this kind. We receive a desirable menu of choice *because* many cultural producers and consumers place intrinsic value on difference. Their creative spirit is driven by identity, and they believe that more matters than just the menu of choice. Similarly, many successful artistic ethoses place numerous values above liberty and freedom of choice, if they value liberty at all.

The cosmopolitan view is committed to regarding these preferences, and these ethoses, as useful false illusions. They are forms of cultural "chauvinism" that, however noble or creativity-enhancing, are fundamentally false as an account of the world. In this account, society would be culturally poorer if the truth were revealed. If everyone believed that cultural identity had instrumental value only, as that view is described above, trade would homogenize to a greater degree. A significant wellspring of human creativity would dry up.

## ■ The Defense of the Particular

Many commentators are not, in reality, strongly attached to cultural diversity as a value, whether it be diversity within societies or across societies. Rather they favor designated manifestations of diversity, as determined by their preferences. They grant special status to particular cultures and time periods; they adore "Breton as it was before the War" or "Bali as it was in 1968." Whatever the pro-diversity rhetoric, the true attachments of these individuals lie elsewhere. They find cross-cultural exchange problematic because it imposes a logic of change on all participating cultures and does not grant special status to their favorites.

Gandhi does not seem to have minded cultural imperialism per se. Rather, he objected when the British altered his favored culture. Although Gandhi complained that British imports were damaging the Indian textile industry, Indian producers had practiced a comparable form of cultural imperialism for centuries. The Indians flooded southeast Asia with their high-quality textile products, starting as early as the first century A.D. and continuing through the present day. India was dominant in the African trade as well, especially after the slave routes opened up. The development of Indian handwoven textiles relied on "exploiting" these external markets.[2]

Indian penetration of other Asian markets was so strong that some of them erected import barriers against the Indian products. Thailand, for instance, enforced import restrictions and sumptuary laws to the detriment of the Indian trade. The British had once sought protection against Indian cloth as well. In the eighteenth century, Indian cloth was greatly popular in Britain. Hand-painted cotton chintz was very popular in European markets, especially in England, and revolutionized European textile styles. An English ban on chintz failed to keep the product out, just as a "buy domestic cloth" movement, an English precursor of Gandhi's Swadeshi movement, failed. The textiles were so highly demanded that they entered England through the Netherlands. These forms of cultural imperialism, as practiced by Indians, supported the industries that Gandhi later claimed were victimized by British cultural imperialism.[3]

The very notion of Gandhi's Swadeshi movement was based on foreign influences. The Swadeshi writers had been strongly influenced by John Ruskin, William Morris, and the nineteenth-century Arts and Crafts movement of Great Britain. These individuals decried the effects of commerce on art and called for a return to the indigenous production of national handicrafts. Yet the Arts and Crafts movement borrowed from foreign influences heavily. William

[2] See, for instance, Chaudhuri (1978, pp. 237, 277), and Guy (1998, p. 10).
[3] On the decline of Indian muslin, see Farnie (1979, p. 99).

Morris, who produced some of the finest carpets in British history, looked to Persian weaving for inspiration about design.[4]

Critics sometimes betray their particularist agendas by invoking the diversity concept inconsistently. For instance, commentators frequently object when the production of a cultural form is clustered in a single region. The United States is by far the world's largest producer and exporter of movies, measured in dollar volume. The critics, however, want other countries to have larger movie industries.

Other times commentators object when a cultural form becomes *less* clustered in a single country or region. When Paul Simon drew on South African music (*mbaqanga*) for his *Graceland* album, he was charged with cultural imperialism. The spread of South African styles to North America, and their subsequent alteration in the hands of Simon, was considered undesirable. In the eyes of these critics, the global spread of the style was associated with exploitation and inauthenticity: not every country should have its own sector for making mbaqanga music. Moviemaking should spread to many countries, and develop in diverse national directions, even if mbaqanga should not.[5]

It is difficult to avoid the conclusion that these critics do not have diversity per se as their primary concern, if diversity is truly a concern at all. Rather, these critics favor or disfavor cultural trends for particular social and aesthetic reasons, and they adapt their rhetorical notion of diversity accordingly, to praise or condemn as they see fit. They favor the exact form that diversity takes in a particular era, without necessarily favoring diversity more generally. The globalization debate nominally concerns diversity in the general sense, but most of the emotion in the debate derives from strong feelings about how things should or should not be, namely particularism.

The distinction between diversity at any single point in time and *diversity across time* further illuminates the particularist nature

---

[4] See Cohn (1989, p. 343), and Haslam (1991, pp. 11, 13, 56, 62–63, 104).

[5] For a sample of negative reactions to *Graceland*, see Louise Meintjes (1990). One of the protests against Simon was violent: on the eve of Simon's 1992 South African

of many complaints. The embrace of particularism, by attempting to freeze cultures in specified historical eras, such as "Bali as it was in 1968," limits diversity across time. A culture, if allowed to evolve, will develop many different forms over decades and centuries. Speeding up the pace of change, as modernity is so often accused of doing, furthers intertemporal diversity. Trade brings change rather than stasis, yet for most critics this form of diversity does not seem to count as a positive.

Critics of cross-cultural exchange face an awkward question. If diversity at any point in time is desirable, why is intertemporal diversity not desirable as well? *Inter*temporal diversity, like *intra*temporal diversity, contributes to experimentation and to whatever intrinsic value variety may possess. Intertemporal diversity also increases the menu of choice, at least insofar as cultural goods are durable and reproducible over time, and thus serves as a potent engine of variety.

Intertemporal diversity does, of course, rend many individuals out of the social fabrics and cultural fabrics they grew up with. The Irish grandmother can no longer converse in Gaelic with most of her grandchildren. The grandchildren will never know the culture that they are missing, and in that regard they will never have a fully informed choice. Many French want their country to have fewer Hollywood movies and more, successful Gallic films.

These frustrations, which may become tragedies in extreme cases, should be taken seriously in any assessment of cross-cultural exchange. Invoking an absolute "right" to one's original culture involves too strong a moral claim, given that cultures are both synthetic and ever changing. The real problem is usually that the younger generation wants a different culture than do the elders. In this case a group right to keep a particular culture would mean a right to prevent the young from making their own choices. So the language of rights does not seem to apply well here.[6]

---

tour (after the cultural boycott had been lifted), one radical anti-apartheid group bombed the offices of the promoter and the sound company.

[6] For one view of minority cultural rights, see Kymlicka (1995).

Nonetheless there is something undesirable, something costly, about the cultural denials brought by cross-cultural exchange. Human beings have strong desires for particular kinds of cultural experience, and globalization thwarts many of these desires on a regular basis.

These examples probably bring us closest to identifying what the debates about globalization are really about. On one side of the ledger stands the wonderfully diverse menu of choice that globalization tends to bring. On the other side of the ledger stand human concerns for particular cultural and social values, and for the distinct national, regional, or tribal identities of numerous individuals. Even when globalization supports relevant measures of diversity, it makes many individuals unhappy about the particular outcomes it generates.

## ■ What Is a Culture?

The strong desire of individuals to maintain a national, regional, or tribal culture raises the question of what such a culture consists of. Why do individuals latch on to some cultural elements as comprising distinct markers of identity and meaning, while attaching little significance to other markers? If all culture is truly synthetic, how much respect should be paid to arbitrary markers of national or regional cultural identity? There are no easy answers to these questions.

The French identify closely with their cinema, but in fact French movies have never been a culturally pure, Gallic product. Foreigners not only influenced many of the best-known "French" films, but they also directed them. *The Passion of Joan of Arc* (1928), probably the most renowned French silent movie, was directed by a Dane, Carl Dreyer. Russian refugees from the Bolshevik revolution moved to France and left a profound imprint on French silent filmmaking. Moving to the sound era, *L'Age d'or, Andalusian Dog, Belle du Jour,* and *The Discreet Charm of the Bourgeoisie*—all French cinematic classics—were directed by Luis Buñuel, a Spaniard. The German Max

Ophüls directed four of his best films in France, including the renowned *The Earrings of Madame D.* The fascist, Vichy propaganda of World War II hit on a truth when it criticized the cosmopolitan nature of French cinema. One French Nazi was exaggerating, but nonetheless reflecting a real truth, when he charged: "Eighty percent of all film personnel are Jewish, 10% emigres without papers, and 10% French, but with Marxist or masonic links; and that's not counting the actors, of whom half are of foreign extraction—Russian, Romanian, Italian, American, Swiss, Belgian—the exact statistical state of the cinema we speak of as 'French.'"[7]

Ironically, significant film protectionism was put into place only when France lost her national independence in the Second World War. The Vichy government enacted film quotas and subsidies to restructure the French economy and as a means of censorship. At the same time, the Vichy government banned American movies, to keep out cultural corruption and to benefit native French producers. These interventions were patterned explicitly on Nazi policies. To further the irony, after the Liberation the French government kept most of the Vichy cinematic institutions, again in the name of protecting French national identity. The French postwar system of cinematic regulation and subsidization was taken directly from the fascist occupation, with changes in emphasis only. So began the system that is now proclaimed as protecting "national French identity."[8]

It is common for culturally synthetic products to become adopted as nationalist emblems. In the late nineteenth century, many Germans objected to soccer on the grounds that it was "English" and "sport" rather than gymnastics; an emotional debate raged at the time.[9] In more recent times most Germans have considered soccer to be a source of national identification and pride.

---

[7] Cited in Crisp (1993, p. 187). On the role of the Russian silent directors, see Crisp (1993, pp. 167–68).

[8] On the Vichy roots of French postwar cinematic policy, see Williams (1992, pp. 276–77, chap. 10), and Crisp (1993, pp. 64–65). On the regulatory body COIC, see Williams (1992, pp. 249–51), and Ehrlich (1985, p. 25, passim). On restrictions on American films, see Armes (1985, chap. 8, and p. 125).

[9] Noam (1991, p. 23).

Many South Africans are very proud of the musical forms that Paul Simon drew on for his *Graceland* album. Yet South African music has borrowed heavily from Western popular music. The mbaqanga music of South Africa is a foot-stomping dance music with accordion and a thumping bass; it does not resemble traditional African music at all, but stands closer to an early, jazzy prototype of rock and roll. Ironically, the charges of musical exploitation and corruption leveled against Simon were once slung at the mbaqanga music he adapted. Both South Africans and foreigners accused mbaqanga music of being a cheap commercial corruption of Western swing and jazz. Musicologist David Rycroft objected because mbaqanga was not "tribal," and because it borrowed so heavily from commercialized American pop. Other academics considered it a watered-down form of Western jazz, a "pallid imitation of American models." The name mbaqanga itself refers to a hastily made mealie bread, carrying the secondary meaning of "a quick buck." South African choral music, as performed by Ladysmith Black Mambazo, drew heavily on Western gospel, spirituals, and minstrel music. All of these foreign forms were introduced to the South African townships earlier in this century, through the gramophone, the radio, and by touring American groups. Paul Simon found South African music so revelatory precisely because it shared so many sources with his own synthesis of the Western pop tradition.[10]

Anecdotes of this kind raise the question of why a nation, region, or tribe should provide the relevant unit of cultural identification. We search in vain to find national cultural contributions that are pure or close to pure in their origins or their nature. Individuals nonetheless identify with specified artistic creations as carriers of national or cultural identities.

Some external influences, such as the early contribution of Russians to French cinema, are absorbed and subsequently treated as

---

[10] On the origins of mbaqanga, see Bergman (1985, chapter 7). On opposition to mbaqanga, see Andersson (1981, pp. 26–27), and Stapledon and May (1987, p. 25). On the early years of South African music, see the Andersson (1981, p. 23). On the origins of South African music, see also Ballantine (1993).

part of the national French heritage. Congo citizens treat Zairean music as their own, despite the significant Cuban input and the Western origin of the electric guitar. Once a culture accepts an item or practice, it loses interest in whether that item or practice was originally foreign. The item or practice becomes regarded as part of the "native" culture. Other influences, such as Hollywood movies in France, remain outside the circle of universal acceptability and continue to be viewed as alien.

We find no obvious principle of demarcation to predict which external influences will be accepted and which will continue to be classified as harmful intrusions. Citizens or cultural members apply complex principles of individuation to foreign innovations, thereby classifying them into the "worrisome" and "not worrisome" categories.

Time is one relevant factor behind the classification. The printing press was brought to the West in the fifteenth century by Gutenberg, but no one regards it today as a carrier of German (or Chinese) cultural imperialism. Its national origins are far removed from its current meaning and functions. Nor do Westerners fear the "excessive" Greek influence on Western philosophy.

Yet the passage of time does not explain most of the distinctions we observe. It is scant comfort to the Canadians that Hollywood has dominated their market for many decades, and has contributed to shaping the Canadian personality for a long time. In contrast, the synthesizer has been widely used in African music only recently, yet it is now considered consonant with the African nature of the music as a whole. In many cases individuals do not even think about how long ago a cultural practice entered their society.

Many foreign influences are judged by their ability to be incorporated and synthesized into a native culture. Individuals will be more likely to accept foreign imports that support or complement what they already have. The violin is an accepted part of Indian classical music, rather than being seen as a harbinger of cultural imperialism.

In the years of silent moviemaking, the Japanese rarely complained about Hollywood cultural imperialism, unlike most other countries. Their *benshi* system used a live narrator to accompany silent films, adding narration and interpretation as the movie proceeded; in this manner film was brought closer to the Kabuki and Noh dramatic traditions. One commentator noted: "[The benshi] exerted as much power over the finished look of a film as any of the production companies, if not more."[11]

In the world of filmmaking, however, such examples are rare. Hollywood movies may influence a native moviemaking style, but the imported film cannot be meaningfully reedited or remade into a synthetic product. And many Hollywood movies, especially the blockbusters, cannot always spawn domestic counterparts, due to the expenses of celebrities, lavish sets, and special effects. This is one reason why cinematic imperialism is such a hot issue. Many cultures cannot easily synthesize the imported product, which thus maintains an appearance of being foreign and intrusive.

We nonetheless find other cases where nonintegratable products win cultural acceptance outside their place of origin. The preponderance of French paintings in top blockbuster exhibits has not produced significant consternation among Americans and other nationalities. While there is an American school of Impressionism derived from French influences, it plays little role in explaining the American acceptance of French painting. German and Austrian composers dominate the classical concert arena in most countries, but this does not occasion charges of cultural imperialism. Nor are the scores of Beethoven symphonies commonly "remixed" by French or American conductors to form a synthetic product. Instead, Beethoven is embraced as part of a more general European and Western heritage, whereas Hollywood is not.

Some distinctions between acceptable and unacceptable foreign influences are based on public agreement alone. That is, citizens develop common markers of what constitutes their culture, and then become sensitive to the loss or depreciation of these markers. These markers do not differ objectively from other features of the culture,

---

[11] The quotation is from Komatsu (1997, p. 178). See also J. Anderson (1992).

nor are they less synthetic. The only difference is that everyone has agreed to make them points of consensus. In that sense the markers are arbitrary; they are simply whatever people can agree on. To some extent, the French tacitly have agreed to make their cinematic heritage a more important marker than their heritage in classical music; therefore they resent Hollywood imports more than they resent Beethoven in the concert hall.

The more "public" art forms often involve greater sensitivity to foreign influence. If an American fast-food chain opens in the central square of a traditional German town, its presence is obvious. Not only does everyone know it is there, but everyone knows that everyone knows it is there. Its presence is common knowledge. Other cultural markers are less prominent. If each wealthy German hires an Italian interior decorator, or hangs a French painting over his or her fireplace, the symbolism is more private and more ambiguous. The Germans need not publicly affirm that they are preferring some other culture over their own.

Nations or regions respond negatively to those foreign influences that expose or reflect their deeper insecurities. France was the world cultural leader before the United States attained this role, and resents having lost the position. The Canadians fear that they do not differ much from the Americans, an anxiety which is driven home daily by the ubiquity and popularity of American culture in Canada. American culture receives tough treatment from many critics simply because America is the world's wealthiest and most powerful nation.

The most culturally synthetic countries often have the hardest time accepting libertarian attitudes. Canada is a hotbed of cultural protectionism in the theoretical realm, but historically the region has shown an amazing ability to change, adapt, and reinvent its culture, drawing heavily on foreign influences. The original idea of the Confederation was an alliance of British and French cultures, transplanted to the New World. Today, only a century and several decades later, at least 40 percent of Canadians are not of French or British origin (depending on how we measure ethnicity). Hungarians, Indians, and Trinidadians are prominent in Toronto, among many others. Ukrainians and Germans settled Manitoba and Saskatchewan. Chinese and other Asians comprise a large share of British Columbia. Vietnamese food can be found in many small Canadian communities, not just in the large cities. The Inuit and Indian influences have resurfaced strongly in recent years. Most Canadians live within one hundred miles of the border with the United States, and, despite their complaints, accept a degree of American influence that can only be described as rampant.

Politics often drives the hostility to particular manifestations of an external culture. The French government, whether in movies, music, or architecture, attempts to impose an elitist Parisian insider culture on the rest of the nation. The supposed fight to keep global diversity is, in part, a fight to limit French cultural diversity. American culture threatens Parisian hegemony over the provinces. More generally, stronger global ties have encouraged political separatism among European minorities. Free access to the world releases the peripheries from the grasp of the local political and cultural center.

The English-speaking Canadians from Ontario are most afraid of American influence, which endangers their leading place in the Canadian federation. The Québécois, separated from America by the French language and a special ethnic heritage, feel less threatened. On the other hand, many Québécois fear French culture, however much they pretend to have constructed a Francophone pan-Atlantic alliance. The French-speaking Acadians of New Brunswick fear the Québécois. Canadian cultural protectionism is motivated not only by external struggles but also by internal politics.

Some individuals object to cultural dilution per se beyond a certain point. They would rather have a larger personal stake in something closer to them, rather than a smaller personal stake in something that is grander but also more distant. For this reason, transparently synthetic cultural products often command less support than is merited by their quality. We can see a personal analog to this fear of dilution. Many individuals seek fame and recognition for their personal achievements. They want to be known for what they have achieved "under their name." They are less keen on being recognized abstractly, as "one of the many who contributed to the glories of Western civilization."[12]

G.F.W. Hegel adopted a universalist perspective when he wrote, "The individual national spirit fulfills itself by merging with the principle of another nation." The cosmopolitan may regard this process with delight, but such an outcome would not occasion widespread celebration in most quarters, whatever its positive consequences for freedom of choice.[13]

Few individuals, even cosmopolitanites, can avoid the intuition that there is something intrinsically troubling about dilution, if they are pressed sufficiently far. The fiction of Octavia Butler provides a scary vision that should give pause to proponents of cross-cultural exchange. Butler's popular science fiction trilogy *Xenogenesis* postulates a race of alien beings, the Oankali, who combine their genetic material with species from other planets. Appropriately, the Oankali are referred to repeatedly as "traders." The plot is based on the premise that the Oankali plan to mix with the human race and create a new, hybrid species on earth. Although the previous humans have virtually destroyed themselves through war, the surviving members of the human race resist this plan strongly, fearing for the identity of their race and for the identities of their potentially hybrid children.

The reader reacts to the Oankali plan with discomfort, just as the humans in the book react. Yet the alien race, despite a variety of failings, is portrayed as no less ethical or noble than the human beings. The synthesis will give the new, hybrid race many strengths

[12] The objection to cultural dilution may have roots in evolutionary biology. Most people feel intuitively that their influence on the world, as produced through their children, diminishes with the passing of generations. Their children have one-half of their genes, their grandchildren one-quarter of their genes, great-grandchildren one-eighth, and so on. Yet the total genetic influence of the parent may well have gone up, if his or her descendents have produced enough offspring. Nonetheless, whether rational or not, many people identify more closely with one child than with four great-grandchildren, even if the total transmitted genetic material is the same. If nothing else, we can more readily observe our genetic contribution to our direct descendants.

[13] See Hegel (1975 [1837], pp. 56, 60).

that current humans do not possess, and eliminate some weaknesses. When pondering this plan, it is no comfort to realize that the human race is the product of many different kinds of genetic material from the past. We react to the Oankali plan with discomfort because we attach intrinsic importance to the current identity of the human race, and we would fear losing that identity. Few individuals are willing to countenance cultural dilutions across all margins, even when they can perceive significant benefits to such dilution. Critiques of human genetic engineering reflect similar fears, even when beneficial improvements are expected.

## ▬ What Conclusions Can Be Drawn?

We see numerous reasons why people in a culture object to some foreign intrusions while ignoring others. None of these differentiations are based fully in logic, nor do they follow any simple rules. Many of the differentiations appear rooted in pride, though it remains unclear why people take pride in some synthetic products and not others. So we are again led back to the view that many of the critics of globalization are focused on particular cultural agendas, rather than advocating a well-defined notion of diversity or holding cultural choice as their primary concern.

Cross-cultural exchange brings a clash of values and priorities that are not susceptible to easy scientific resolution. Nonetheless I am fundamentally sympathetic to the extension of markets across geographic regions, without denying the difficulty of adjudicating the resulting discord of values.

We should consider the cautious embrace of a cosmopolitan multiculturalism as a guiding aesthetic principle and as a practical guide to policy. The arts, at their best, help us see the world anew, lose our immediate and more mundane concerns, and be swept up in a tide of aesthetic ecstasy. Cosmopolitanism suggests that these ends ought to stand above the concrete details of politics, national borders, regional sympathies, and tribal loyalties.

Rudolf Rocker, in his neglected 1937 book *Nationalism and Culture*, argued that culture is a synthetic and cosmopolitan product of voluntary exchanges among free individuals. In his view freedom encourages creativity, while cultural nationalism leads to stifling governmental control. Even if we reject some of Rocker's more extreme claims about the failures of government, most cultural innovations are far more synthetic than most individuals realize. Furthermore, the counterexamples against cross-cultural exchange, such as Hollywood's strong presence in world cinematic markets or the modern fate of Indian handweaving, merit a more positive slant than they often receive, as I have tried to argue in earlier chapters.

As an ethical ideal, cosmopolitanism has a long and noble philosophic tradition, starting with the Roman Stoics and running through such modern writers as David Hollinger and Jeremy Waldron. Erik Satie remarked aptly that "art has no country." Diogenes announced proudly, "I am a citizen of the world." More recently, Paul Simon proclaimed, "You can't stop music at a border." These brief pronouncements, though bereft of analysis, ring fundamentally true.[14]

The principle of free speech suggests also that we should not try to thwart cultural exchange. Most intellectuals claim a strong adherence to free speech and would ardently protest if their domestic government tried to censor a book or movie. These same individuals often react with equanimity, or *approval*, when a foreign government tries to keep out American films, as South Korea has done, or the cheaper American edition of a book, as Australia has done. The principle of free speech applies to those cases no less. Whether or not we think the case for free speech is absolute, I see the burden of proof as lying on those who seek to violate free-speech rights, rather than on those who wish to preserve them.

In embracing such a "free speech cosmopolitanism," we must confront at least three potentially or ostensibly clashing values: the "paradox of diversity," the strong preferences of many individuals for particular markers of cultural identity, and the common desire for cultural difference and distinction. I will consider each in turn.

---

[14] Satie is cited in Richards (1996b, p. 63). See also Diogenes Laertius (1965, p. 65). On Simon, see Humphries (1989, p. 143).

The paradox of diversity, as discussed in the third chapter on ethos and the tragedy of cultural loss, noted a counterintuitive possibility; namely, the world as a whole may be more diverse if some societies refuse to accept diversity as a value. Those cultures will continue to generate highly unique creations, given their status as cultural outliers.

It is plausible that the paradox of diversity holds for some but not all social changes (some manifestations of wealth and technology increase diversity across the board; see chapter 2). When the paradox operates, however, additional cross-cultural contact will cause the menu of global choice to decline. In these cases we can no longer rely on the menu-of-choice argument to provide an absolutely secure defense of cosmopolitanism.

Cosmopolitanism must resort to a value judgment to overcome the force of this critique. I will define this value judgment as the view that poorer societies should not be required to serve as *diversity slaves*.

Note that when trade spreads to lesser-developed or poorer societies, diversity likely increases *within those societies*. Individuals will have more to choose from than in the past, and they will be happy to have those choices. A brief visit to a Wal-mart in Mexico will confirm this truth. Insofar as anyone feels the loss of diversity, it is the richer countries. Bringing a shopping mall to Papua New Guinea gives the Papuans more choice, but it may give the American collector of Papuan sculpture less choice, if it weakens the inspiration behind those sculptures by changing the underlying social ethos.

If we reject the premise that poorer societies should be diversity slaves, we will tend to see this trade-off as desirable, all things considered. The Papuans gain diversity of choice and the Western collectors and museum-goers lose diversity of choice. Insofar as we see the Papuan gain as somehow "greater" or "more important" than the American loss, the case for trade will remain. Invoking this value judgment allows cosmopolitanism to stand, undefeated by the paradox of diversity, if not completely unscathed.

In this context, cosmopolitanism looks even better if we focus on operative diversity in the world, rather than objective diversity. To whatever extent the world was diverse in 1450, few individuals were able to enjoy or appreciate that diversity. No one had any idea how diverse the world was, and it is unclear how much most people would have cared, had they known. Today a large number of people are aware of world diversity and use it to enrich many areas of our lives, as I have stressed throughout this book. Modernity allows us to enjoy the diversity of the world to a very high degree, relative to previous ages, even when it undercuts that diversity in some regards.

The second value that potentially clashes with cross-cultural exchange is more psychological in nature. The mere fact of *change* will produce serious disappointment for individuals who seek to preserve particular markers of cultural identity.

On this point cross-cultural exchange fares better than is frequently recognized. The above discussion in this chapter suggests that markers of national, regional, and tribal identities are adjustable to a considerable degree. This is not to deny that markers are needed; cultural identity is a vital part of our lives. Nonetheless it is not obvious why the markers from the past should have more normative force than other possible markers. If cross-cultural exchange replaces an old set of markers with a new set, perhaps this should not be intrinsic cause for concern. Identity markers change over time in any case, and they are never governed by fully rational processes.

Such an attitude does not ignore the fact that many people prefer the old markers, perhaps ardently. Cosmopolitanism is problematic to the extent it must take up a position against the net weight of human preferences.

In reality, however, cultural clash arises in the first place only because many people wish to shift cultural markers, create new ones, or share cultural markers with new and broader communities. Most modern Irish prefer to speak English—the language of Shakespeare and Joyce—rather than Gaelic. High school girls in Thailand wish to share the cultural marker of Madonna with their peers abroad. One Frenchman remarked, "[I] remain fascinated by America. . . . I am convinced that [the ideas of] Merleau-Ponty are still of value, but tomorrow I am going to Euro Disneyland."[15]

So a respect for human preferences does not dictate that we stick with the earlier cultural markers, or assign them special priority. Preferences change over time and differ across individuals. Nor do we have any tractable metric for determining whether the new markers are preferred to the old. The difference in preferences often spans the generations, with the relatively young driving the change and the relatively old resisting it. There may be no common framework in which the competing aesthetic claims can be adjudicated, although a free-speech presumption would again favor the cosmopolitan perspective.[16]

We also know that economic development brings heterogenization and homogenization at the same time. It expands the size of markets and tends to increase the menu of choice. The overall menu of potential markers therefore is likely to increase rather than shrink. While it is difficult to argue that the new markers will be better than the old, we should not expect them to be worse.

On the issue of cultural markers, cross-cultural exchange therefore fights to a draw. It brings a change that is neither definitely an improvement nor definitely a cost. Such a draw, however, may be all that globalization needs, given its successful record in augmenting the overall menu of choice and the free-speech presumption in its favor.

The third value that potentially clashes with cross-cultural exchange, the desire for difference and distinction, can be treated with

---

[15] Kuisel (1993, p. 230).

[16] The economists' standard of cost-benefit analysis does us little good here. Normative economic models judge policies in terms of individual preferences, which are usually treated as fixed and unchanging. Here the very question is what kinds of preferences will be encouraged in the subsequent development of a culture. Furthermore, economic models assume that the willingness to pay for a change is roughly equivalent to the willingness to be paid for not having it. Cultural defenders may not have so much money to pay to defend their prize, but sometimes they would not give it up for any amount of money in the world.

similar arguments. Trade is a controversial issue because citizens disagree about how much commonality and how much distinction a country should have at a global level. Some individuals seek more distinction and difference for their societies, others prefer to have more in common with the broader global community. Again, cross-cultural exchange does no better than to reach a draw on this issue, since we cannot easily adjudicate the competing perspectives, but a draw is all that is needed.

The question also remains whether it is the *objective* or *subjective* metric of difference that should matter for our assessment. In terms of objective lists of available goods and services, societies are becoming more alike in the sense of sharing a common diversity. Yet the subjective perception of difference influences human welfare at least as much. Canadians have no difficulty feeling very different from Americans, even though to the rest of the world the United States and Canada are remarkably alike, at least for two disparate nations. So many Canadians wear their flag on their backpacks when traveling because otherwise they will be mistaken for Americans. Analogous observations can be made for Australia and New Zealand, or Germany and Switzerland; in each case, growing objective similarities have been accompanied by greater subjective feelings of difference, if only by highlighting the remaining contrasts. While sixteenth-century Swiss undoubtedly felt different from the Germans, the feeling was a less active one, if only because they had less contact, given the higher cost of transportation and communications. Today border crossings, and other forms of cross-cultural contact, are much more common, and so are subjective feelings of difference.

Which aspects of the preference for difference should receive weight? If we wish to maximize how much people *feel* different from others, cross-cultural exchange is remarkably well suited to achieve this end. Boosting immigration quotas, for instance, would spur this feeling quickly, as does cheap travel.

More plausibly, people do not enjoy feeling different from other cultures in the same way that they enjoy eating ice cream. The feeling of difference is not an intrinsic source of pleasure for them. More likely, the talk of "difference" is a code word for some deeper set of preferences over cultural values. Individuals may value holding the kinds of identity that cause the difference—such as deep attachments to their place of birth—without valuing difference per se. In other cases, many Frenchmen simply object to the American lifestyle. They would happily be more like the Americans, if it were on their own terms, with the Americans adopting the best of French culture. These individuals also do not care about cultural difference per se. They might be quite happy, for instance, if the rest of the world adopted French as its language of diplomacy or high finance.

Therefore the value of diversity across societies, more often than not, once again boils down to a desire for particular cultural markers. We have already seen that cultural trade at least fights to a draw on this question.[17]

Now, however, comes a more difficult truth for cosmopolitan multiculturalism. At repeated points, we have seen that trade supports diversity within society, but partly because cultural creators do not hold fully cosmopolitan attitudes. Cosmopolitan attitudes, if held fully and consistently, would defeat the cosmopolitan end of diversity and freedom of choice. In similar fashion, we can say that the stock market operates with a relative degree of efficiency only because many investors—probably most investors—believe it is inefficient and thus spend time trying to find bargains.

Given these paradoxes, cosmopolitanism has two choices. It can proclaim the desirability of universal cosmopolitan belief and try to

---

[17] Whether the diversity of market multiculturalism would lead to ethnic fragmentation and political instability lies beyond the scope of this book. Samuel Huntingdon, in his *The Clash of Civilizations* (1996), charges that the world can expect warfare between disparate cultures; Benjamin Barber echoes a related fear in his *Jihad vs. McWorld* (1995). At least on the surface we have no reason that globalization will bring more political chaos. Globalization, by limiting the number of truly distinct societies, may help cultures to understand each other. Furthermore, the complementary growth of homogenization and heterogenization in tandem can limit fragmentation. The homogenizing aspects of globalization can give cultures more common points of reference, while at the same time they become more diverse within. Finally,

live with the cultural consequences. We would then have to assess whether the bargain was worth it.

Alternatively, cosmopolitanism could become a furtive cultural critique, a framework for judging political and cultural developments, but without offering an independent reform proposal on the macro scale. In terms of individual attitudes, a bit more cosmopolitanism might be desirable, but not too much. This version of cosmopolitanism would recognize the inevitability (and desirability) of noncosmopolitan belief in the cultural realm, but nonetheless would view such beliefs as the source of excess cultural insulation and protectionism.

Instead of this halfway attitude, some cosmopolitans wish for creativity-enhancing beliefs in the cultural realm, but liberty-enhancing beliefs in the political realm. Many libertarians, for instance, advocate a world where individuals value their cultural identities fiercely, yet without wishing to impose such beliefs on others or without granting those identities favored protection in the broader market for cultural competition.

Such a view, while it outlines an attractive-sounding ideal, begs the question. Even if this state of affairs were desirable, such bifurcated beliefs are not generally possible in a diverse world. Not many cultures, if any, can accommodate or support this set of beliefs on a wide scale. Only Western societies of a very particular kind draw such a clear distinction between the realm of coercion and the realm of voluntary interaction; even in the United States only a small number of libertarians do. Such beliefs will not be universal or even necessarily widespread in a diverse world. Wishing for this set of beliefs is, in essence, wishing for the proverbial free lunch that, in other contexts, libertarians insist does not exist.

Given that the potential for such beliefs is problematic in a diverse world, the resulting cosmopolitanism must take on a strange

---

the evidence suggests that economically free societies tend to have less trouble with diversity and ethnic conflict (Sadowski 1998, p. 117); in this regard free trade in culture may help stability rather than harming it.

character. It is an attitude and a wish that is one step removed from the feasible. It is a way of appreciating the irrational longing for the particular, and its resulting aesthetic benefits, while at the same time holding such longings at a distance on a higher theoretical level. This cosmopolitanism provides a metaperspective on the evolution of contemporary culture, just as Hegel sought to illuminate his own era. Unlike for Hegel, however, the truth can never be brought into the full awareness of those participating in the historical process. Cosmopolitanism is a secret account of our numerous and impressive cultural successes, but an account that dare not see the complete light of day.

# References

Abel, Richard. 1984. *French Cinema, The First Wave, 1915–1929*. Princeton: Princeton University Press.

———. 1994. *The Ciné Goes to Town: French Cinema 1896–1914*. Berkeley: University of California Press.

———. 1999. *The Red Rooster Scare: Making Cinema American, 1900–1910*. Berkeley: University of California Press.

Allane, Lee. 1988. *Oriental Rugs: A Buyer's Guide*. London: Thames and Hudson.

Allen, Robert C. 1996. "As the World Turns: Television Soap Operas and Global Media Culture." In *Mass Media and Free Trade: NAFTA and Cultural Industries*, edited by Emile G. McAnany and Kenton T. Wilkinson, 110–30. Austin: University of Texas Press.

Almquist, Alden. 1993. "The Society and Its Environment." In *Zaire: A Country Study*, edited by Sandra W. Meditz and Tim Merrill, 61–134. Washington, D.C.: Library of Congress.

Amith, Jonathan. 1995. *The Amate Tradition: Innovation and Dissent in Mexican Art*, edited by Jonathan Amith. Chicago: Mexican Fine Arts Center Museum.

Amsden, Charles Avery. 1972. *Navaho Weaving: Its Technic and History*. Glorieta, N.M.: Rio Grande Press.

Anderson, E. N. 1988. *The Food of China*. New Haven: Yale University Press.

Anderson, Joseph L. 1992. "Spoken Silents in the Japanese Cinema; or, Talking to Pictures: Essaying the *Katsuben*, Contextualizing the Texts." In *Reframing Japanese Cinema: Authorship, Genre, and History*, edited by Arthur Nolletti Jr. and David Desser, 259–311. Bloomington: Indiana University Press.

Anderson, Joseph L., and Donald Richie. 1959. *The Japanese Film: Art and Industry.* Rutland, V.T.: Charles E. Tuttle Company.

Andersson, Muff. 1981. *Music in the Mix: The Story of South African Popular Music.* Johannesburg: Ravan Press.

Andrew, Dudley. "Sound in France: The Origins of a Native School." In *Rediscovering French Film*, edited by Mary Lea Bandy, 57–66. New York: Museum of Modern Art, 1983.

Anstey, Vera. 1936. *The Economic Development of India.* London: Longmans, Green, and Co.

Appadurai, Arjun. 1996. *Modernity at Large: Cultural Dimensions of Globalization.* Minneapolis: University of Minnesota Press.

Appiah, Kwame Anthony. 1992. *In My Father's House: Africa in the Philosophy of Culture.* New York: Oxford University Press.

———. 1998. "Cosmopolitan Patriots." In *Cosmopolitics: Thinking and Feeling beyond the Nation*, edited by Pheng Cheah and Bruce Robbins, 91–114. Minneapolis: University of Minnesota.

Armes, Roy. 1985. *French Cinema.* New York: Oxford University Press.

———. 1987. *Third World Film-Making and the West.* Berkeley: University of California Press.

Arom, Simha. 1991. *African Polyphony and Polyrhythm: Musical Structure and Methodology.* Cambridge: Cambridge University Press.

Audley, Paul. 1983. *Canada's Cultural Industries: Broadcasting, Publishing, Records and Film.* Toronto: James Lorimer and Company.

Bagchi, Amiya Kumar. 1972. *Private Investment in India 1900–1939.* Cambridge: At the University Press.

Baker, William F., and George Dessart. 1998. *Down the Tube: An Inside Account of the Failure of American Television.* New York: Basic Books.

Bailey, Garrick, and Roberta Glenn Bailey. 1986. *A History of the Navajos: The Reservation Years.* Santa Fe: School of American Research Press.

Baker, Christopher John. 1984. *An Indian Rural Economy 1880–1955: The Tamilnad Countryside.* Oxford: Clarendon Press.

Baker, Patricia L. 1995. *Islamic Textiles.* London: British Museum Press.

Ballantine, Christopher. 1993. *Marabi Nights: Early South African Jazz and Vaudeville.* Johannesburg: Ravan Press.

Barber, Benjamin R. 1995. *Jihad vs. McWorld.* New York: Times Books.

Barlow, Sean; Banning Eyre; and Jack Vartoogian. 1995. *Afropop!: An Illustrated Guide to Contemporary African Music.* Edison, N.J.: Chartwell Books.

Barnard, Nicholas. 1993. *Arts and Crafts of India.* London: Conran Octupus.

Barnet, Richard, and John Cavanagh. 1996. "Homogenization of Global Culture." In *The Case against the Global Economy, and for a Turn towards the*

*Local*, edited by Jerry Mander and Edward Goldsmith, 71–77. San Francisco: Sierra Club Books.

Barnouw, Erik, and S. Krishnaswamy 1963. *Indian Film*. New York: Columbia University Press.

Bascom, William. 1976. *Changing African Art*. Berkeley: University of California Press.

Baskaran, S. Theodore. 1981. *The Message Bearers: Nationalist Politics and the Entertainment Media in South India, 1880–1945*. Madras, India: Cre-A.

Bayley, C. A. 1986. "The Origins of Swadeshi (home industry): Cloth and Indian Society, 1700–1930." In *The Social Life of Things: Commodities in Cultural Perspective*, edited by Arjun Appadurai, 285–321. Cambridge: Cambridge University Press.

Bean, Susan S. 1989. "Gandhi and Khadi, the Fabric of Indian Independence." In *Cloth and Human Experience*, edited by Annette B. Weiner and Jane Schneider, 355–76. Washington, D.C.: Smithsonian Institution Press.

Bell-Villada, Gene H. 1996. *Art for Art's Sake and Literary Life*. Lincoln: University of Nebraska Press.

Bennett, Ian. 1996. *Rugs and Carpets of the World*. Edison, N.J.: Wellfleet Press.

Bergman, Billy. 1985. *Goodtime Kings: Emerging African Pop*. New York: Quill.

Berner, Robert. 1997. "A Holiday Greeting U.S. TV Won't Air: Shoppers Are 'Pigs.'" *Wall Street Journal Europe*, 21–22 November, A1, A2.

Berwanger, Dietrich. 1995. "The Third World." In *Television: An International History*, edited by Anthony Smith, 309–30. Oxford: Oxford University Press.

Blomberg, Nancy J. 1988. *Navajo Textiles*. Tucson: University of Arizona Press.

Boas, George. 1948. *Essays on Primitivism and Related Ideas in the Middle Ages*. Baltimore: Johns Hopkins Press.

Bokelenge, Lonah Malangi. 1986. "Modern Zairean Music: Yesterday, Today, and Tomorrow." In *The Arts and Civilization of Black and African Peoples*, Vol. 1, edited by Joseph Ohiomogben Okpaku, Alfred Esimatemi Opubor, and Benjamin Olatunji Oloruntimehin, 132–51. Lagos, Nigeria: Centre for Black and African Arts and Civilization.

Bordwell, David. 2000. *Planet Hong Kong: Popular Cinema and the Art of Entertainment*. Cambridge: Harvard University Press.

Borpujari, Jitendra G. 1973. "Indian Cottons and the Cotton Famine of 1860–65." *Indian and Social History Review*, 37–49.

Botombele, Bokonga Ekanga. 1976. *Cultural Policy in the Republic of Zaire*. Paris: Unesco Press.

Bourdieu, Pierre. 1986. *Distinction: A Social Critique on the Judgment of Taste*. London: Routledge and Kegan Paul.

Bradley, Lloyd. 1996. *Reggae on CD: The Essential Guide*. London: Kyle Cathie Limited.

Bredemeier, Kenneth. 1999. "Serving up a Medley of Cultures." *Washington Post*, 26 May, E1, E10.

Brody, J. J. 1971. *Indian Painters and White Patrons*. Albuquerque: University of New Mexico Press.

———. 1976. *Between Traditions. Navajo Weaving towards the End of the Nineteenth Century.* Iowa City: University of Iowa Museum of Art.

Brunside, M. 1997. *Spirits of the Passage: The Transatlantic Slave Trade in the Seventeenth Century.* Edited by R. Robotham. New York: Simon and Schuster.

Buchanan, Daniel Houston. 1934. *The Development of Capitalistic Enterprise in India*. New York: Macmillan.

Buell, Frederick. 1994. *National Culture and the New Global System*. Baltimore: Johns Hopkins Press.

Burnett, Robert. 1996. *The Global Jukebox: The International Music Industry.* London: Routledge.

Butler, Octavia. n.d. *Xenogenesis*. New York: Guild America Books.

Campbell, Tyrone; and Joel Kopp; and Kate Kopp. 1991. *Navajo Pictorial Weaving 1880–1950*. New York: Dutton Studio Books.

Canclíni, Nestor Garcia. 1993. *Transforming Modernity: Popular Culture in Mexico*. Austin: University of Texas Press.

———. 1995. *Hybrid Cultures: Strategies for Entering and Leaving Modernity.* Minneapolis: University of Minnesota Press.

Caves, Richard E. 2000. *Creative Industries*. Cambridge: Harvard University Press.

Cerny, Charlene and Suzanne Seriff, eds. 1996. *Recycled, Re-Seen: Folk Art from the Global Scrap Heap*. New York: Harry N. Abrams.

Chakravarty, Sumita S. 1993. *National Identity in Indian Popular Cinema, 1947–1987*. Austin: University of Texas Press.

Chandra, Bipan. 1966. *The Rise and Growth of Economic Nationalism in India*. New Delhi: People's Publishing House.

———. 1968. "Reinterpretations of Nineteenth-Century Indian Economic History." *Indian Economic and Social History Review* 5:35–75.

Chandra, Pramrod. 1981. "The Sculpture and Architecture of Northern India." In *The Arts of India*, edited by Basil Gray, 30–52. Ithaca: Cornell University Press.

Chang, Kevin O'Brien, and Wayne Chen. 1998. *Reggae Routes: The Story of Jamaican Music*. Philadelphia: Temple University Press.

Chaudhuri, K. N. 1978. *The Trading World of Asia and the English East India Company 1660–1760*. Cambridge: Cambridge University Press.

Cheek, Lawrence W. 1996. *Santa Fe*. Oakland: Fodor's Travel Publications.

Christenson, Peter G., and Donald F. Roberts. *It's Not Only Rock And Roll: Popular Music in the Lives of Adolescents*. Cresskill, N.J.: Hampton Press.

Chwe, Michael Suk-Young. 1999. "Game Theory and Global Rituals: Media, McDonald's, and Madonna." Unpublished manuscript, University of Chicago.

Clausen, Christopher. 1981. *The Place of Poetry: Two Centuries of an Art in Crisis*. Lexington, Ky. University Press of Kentucky.

Clifford, James. 1988. *The Predicament of Culture: Twentieth-Century Ethnography, Literature, and Art*. Cambridge: Harvard University Press.

———. 1997. *Routes: Travel and Translation in the Late Twentieth Century*. Cambridge: Harvard University Press.

Coccossis, Harry. 1996. "Tourism and Sustainability: Perspectives and Implications." In *Sustainable Tourism? European Experiences*, edited by Gerda K. Priestly, J. Arwel Edwards, and Harry Coccossis, 1–21. Wallingford, England: CAB International.

Cohn, Bernard. 1989. "Cloth, Clothes, and Colonialism: India in the Nineteenth Century." In *Cloth and Human Experience*, edited by Annette B. Weiner and Jane Schneider, 303–53. Washington, D.C.: Smithsonian Institution Press.

Coles, Janet, and Robert Budwig. 1997. *Beads: An Exploration of Bead Traditions around the World*. New York: Simon and Schuster Editions.

Cooper, Ilay, and John Gillow. 1996. *Arts and Crafts of India*. London: Thames and Hudson.

Cootner, Cathryn. 1981. *Flat-Woven Textiles* Washington, D.C.: The Textile Museum.

Costello, Mark, and David Foster Wallace. 1990. *Signifying Rappers: Rap and Race in the Urban Present*. New York: Ecco Press.

Costigliola, Frank. 1984. *Awkward Dominion: American Political, Economic, and Cultural Relations with Europe, 1919–1933*. Ithaca: Cornell University Press.

Cowen, Tyler. 1996. "Why I Do Not Believe in the Cost-Disease: Comment on Beaumol." *Journal of Cultural Economics* 20, 207–14.

———. 1998. *In Praise of Commercial Culture*. Cambridge: Harvard University Press.

———. 2000. *What Price Fame?* Cambridge: Harvard University Press.

Cowen, Tyler and Robin Grier. 1996. "Does the Artist Suffer from a Cost Disease?" *Rationality and Society* 8, no. 1 (February): 5–24.

Cowen, Tyler, and Eric Crampton. 2001. "Uncommon Culture." *Foreign Policy* (July/August): 28–29.

Crafton, Donald. 1997. *The Talkies: American Cinema's Transition to Sound, 1926–1931*. New York: Charles Scribner's Sons.

Crane, Diana. 1972. *Invisible Colleges: Diffusion of Knowledge in Scientific Communities*. Chicago: University of Chicago Press.

Crisp, Colin. 1993. *The Classic French Cinema, 1930–1960*. Bloomington: University of Indiana Press.

Dale, Martin. 1997. *The Movie Game: The Film Business in Britain, Europe, and America*. London: Cassell.

Damian, Carol. 1995. *The Virgin of the Andes: Art and Ritual in Colonial Cuzco*. Miami Beach: Grassfield Press.

Daniels, Bill; David Leedy; and Steven D. Sills. 1998. *Movie Money: Understanding Hollywood's (Creative) Accounting Practices*. Los Angeles: Silman-James Press.

Danticat, Edwidge, and Jonathan Demme. 1997. *Island on Fire*. Nyack, N.Y.: Kaliko Press.

Danto, Arthur C. 1981. *The Transfiguration of the Commonplace: A Philosophy of Art*. Cambridge: Harvard University Press.

Dedera, Don. 1975. *Navajo Rugs: How to Find, Evaluate, Buy, and Care for Them*. Northland Press.

Deitch, Lewis I. 1989. "The Impact of Tourism on the Arts and Crafts of the Indians of the Southwestern United States." In *Hosts and Guests: The Anthropolgy of Tourism*, edited by Valene L. Smith, 223–35. Philadelphia: University of Pennsylvania Press.

Devine, T. M. 1999. *The Scottish Nation A History, 1700–2000*. New York: Viking.

Dibbets, Karel. 1997. "The Introduction of Sound." In *The Oxford History of World Cinema*, edited by Geoffrey Nowell-Smith, 211–19. Oxford: Oxford University Press.

Diogenes, Laertius. 1925. *Lives of the Philosophers*. Vol. 2. Cambridge: Harvard University Press.

Dissanayake, Wimal. 1988. "Japanese Cinema." In *Cinema and Cultural Identity: Reflections on Films from Japan, India, and China*, edited by Wimal Dissanayake, 15–18. Lanham, Md.: University Press of America.

Dockstader, Frederick J. 1954. *The Kachina and the White Man*. Bloomfield Hills, Mich.: Cranbrook Institute of Science.

Doheny-Farina, Stephen. 1996. *The Wired Neighborhood*. New Haven: Yale University Press.

Drozdiak, William. 1993. "The City of Light, Sans Bright Ideas." *Washington Post*, 28 October, D1, D6.

Dubin, Lois Sher. 1987. *The History of Beads*. New York: Harry N. Abrams.

Duin, Julia. 1999. "Navajos Learn to Keep Rug Art Alive." *Washington Times*, 18 August, A2.

Dunnett, Peter. 1990. *The World Television Industry: An Economic Analysis*. London: Routledge.

Durkheim, Emile. 1964 [1893]. *The Division of Labor*. New York: Free Press.

Dutt, Romesh. 1969 [1904]. *The Economic History of India in the Victorian Age*. New York: Augustus M. Kelley.

Dutta, Krishna, and Andrew Robinson. 1995. *Rabindranath Tagore: The Myriad-Minded Man*. New York: St. Martin's Press.

Edwards, A. Cecil. 1960. *The Persian Carpet: A Survey of the Carpet-Weaving Industry of Persia*. London: Gerald Duckworth.

Egan, Martha J. 1993. *Relicarios: Devotional Miniatures from the Americas*. Santa Fe: Museum of New Mexico Press.

Ehrlich, Evelyn. 1985. *Cinema of Paradox: French Filmmaking under the German Occupation*. New York: Columbia University Press.

Erickson, Lee. 1996. *The Economy of Literary Form: English Literature and the Industrialization of Publishing, 1800–1850*. Baltimore: Johns Hopkins University Press.

Ewens, Graeme. 1991. *Africa O-Ye!*. New York: Da Capo Press.

Fairchild, Hoxie Neale. 1961. *The Noble Savage: A Study in Romantic Naturalism*. New York: Russell and Russell.

Farnie, D. A. 1979. *The English Cotton Industry and the World Market 1815–1896*. Oxford: Clarendon Press.

Feder, Norman. 1971. *Two Hundred Years of North American Indian Art*. New York: Praeger Publishers.

———. 1986. "European Influences on Plains Indian Art." In *The Arts of the North American Indian*, edited by Edwin L. Wade, 93–104. New York: Hudson Hill Press.

Feehan, Fanny. 1981. "Suggested Links between Eastern and Celtic Music." In *The Celtic Consciousness*, edited by Robert O'Driscoll, 333–39. New York: George Braziller.

Feest, Christian F. 1992. *Native Arts of North America*. New York: Thames and Hudson.

Fore, Steve. 1997. "Jackie Chan and the Cultural Dynamics of Global Entertainment." In *Transnational Chinese Cinemas*, edited by Sheldon Hsiao-peng Lu, 239–62. Honolulu: University of Hawaii Press.

Frank, Robert H., and Philip J. Cook. 1995. *The Winner-Take-All Society: How More and More Americans Compete for Ever Fewer and Bigger Prizes, Encouraging Economic Waste, Income Inequality, and an Impoverished Cultural Life*. New York: Free Press.

Friedman, Thomas. 1999. *The Lexus and the Olive Tree*. London: HarperCollins.

French Ministry of Culture (Studies and Research Department). 1970. *Some Aspects of French Cultural Policy*. Paris: UNESCO.

Fuchs, Lawrence H. 1990. *The American Kaleidoscope: Race, Ethnicity, and the Civic Culture*. Hanover, Mass.: University Press of New England.

Furst, Peter T., and Jill L. Furst. 1982. *North American Indian Art*. New York: Artpress Books.

Garncarz, Joseph. 1994. "Hollywood in Germany: The Role of American Films in Germany, 1925–1990." In *Hollywood in Europe: Experiences of a Cultural Hegemony*, 94–135. Amsterdam: VU University Press.

Gioia, Dana. 1992. *Can Poetry Matter? Essays on Poetry and American Culture*. St. Paul: Graywolf Press.

Gittinger, Mattiebelle. 1982. *Master Dyers to the World: Technique and Trade in Early Indian Dyed Cotton Textiles*. Washington, D.C.: The Textile Museum.

Glassie, Henry. 1989. *The Spirit of Folk Art: The Girard Collection at the Museum of International Folk Art*. New York: Harry N. Abrams.

Gokulsing, K. Moti, and Wimal Dissanayake. 1998. *Indian Popular Cinema: A Narrative of Cultural Change*. Oakhill, England: Trentham Books.

Gomery, Douglas. 1985. "Economic Struggle and Hollywood Imperialism: Europe Converts to Sound." In *Film Sound: Theory and Practice*, edited by Elizabeth Weis and John Belton, 25–36. New York: Columbia University Press.

———. 1992. *Shared Pleasures: A History of Movie Presentation in the United States*. Madison: University of Wisconsin Press.

Graham, Ronnie. 1985. "Zaire Sets the Pace." *West Africa*, November, 2268–69.

Grantham, Bill. 2000. *"Some Big Bourgeois Brothel": Contexts for France's Culture Wars with Hollywood*. Luton, England: University of Luton Press.

Gray, John. 1998. *False Dawn: The Delusions of Global Capitalism*. London: Granta Books.

Grimes, William. 1998. "Talk about a Fork in the Road. How and Why Did the French Make an Art of Cuisine While England Descended to Bangers and 'Chip Butty' "? *New York Times*, 9 May, A15, A17.

Guillermoprieto, Alma. 1999. "Cuban Hit Parade." *New York Review of Books* 14 January: 46, no. 1, 34–35.

Guy, John. 1998. *Woven Cargoes: Indian Textiles in the East*. New York: Thames and Hudson.

Haberland, Wolfgang. 1986. "Aesthetics in Native American Art." In *The Arts of the North American Indian*, edited by Edwin L. Wade, 107–31. New York: Hudson Hill Press.

Hall, Peter G. 1998. *Cities in Civilization: Culture, Innovation, and Urban Order*. London: Westfield and Nicholson.

Hannerz, Ulf. 1992. *Cultural Complexity: Studies in the Social Organization of Meaning*. New York: Columbia University Press.

———. 1996. *Transnational Connections: Culture, People, Places*. New York: Routledge.

Harmon, Melissa Burdick. 1998. "Food: A Love Story." *Biography Magazine*, December, 110.

Harrev, Flemming. 1989. "Jambo Records and the Promotion of Popular Music in East Africa: The Story of Otto Larsen and East Africa Records Ltd. 1952–1963." In *Perspectives on African Music*, African Studies Series 9, edited by Wolfgang Bender, 103–37. Bayreuth, Germany: Eckhard Breitinger.

Harris, Henry T. 1908. *Monograph on the Carpet Weaving Industry of Southern India*. Madras: Government Press.

Harris, Jennifer. 1993. *Textiles, 5,000 Years: An International History and Illustrated Survey*. New York: Harry N. Abrams.

Haslam, Malcolm. 1991. *Arts and Crafts Carpets*. New York: Rizzoli.

Hatch, Martin. 1989. "Popular Music in Indonesia." In *World Music, Politics, and Social Change*, edited by Simon Frith, 47–67. Manchester: Manchester University Press.

Hayes, Carlton J. H. 1930. *France: A Nation of Patriots*. New York: Columbia University Press.

Hebdige, Dick. 1990. *Cut 'n' Mix: Culture, Identity, and Caribbean Music*. London: Methuen.

Hegel, George Wilhelm Friedrich. 1975 [1837]. *Lectures on the Philosophy of World History*. Cambridge: Cambridge University Press.

Helfgott, Leonard M. 1994. *Ties That Bind: A Social History of the Iranian Carpet*. Washington, D.C.: Smithsonian Institution Press.

Helpman, Elhanan, and Paul R. Krugman. 1985. *Market Structure and Foreign Trade: Increasing Returns, Imperfect Competition, and the International Economy*. Cambridge: MIT Press.

Herrnstein Smith, Barbara. 1988. *Contingencies of Value: Alternative Perspectives for Critical Theory*. Cambridge: Harvard University Press.

Hessel, Ingo. 1998. *Inuit Art: An Introduction*. New York· Harry N. Abrams.

Hibbert, Christopher. 1969. *The Grand Tour*. New York: G. P. Putnam's Sons.

Hollinger, David A. 1995. *Postethnic America: Beyond Multiculturalism*. New York: Basic Books.

Hooker, Richard J. 1981. *Food and Drink in America: A History*. Indianapolis: Bobbs-Merrill.

Hostetler, John A. 1993. *Amish Society*. Baltimore: Johns Hopkins Press.

Howe, James. 1998. *A People Who Would Not Kneel: Panama, the United States, and the San Blas Kuna*. Washington, D.C.: Smithsonian Institution Press.

Hughes, Robert. 1991. *The Shock of the New: Art and the Century of Change*. London: BBC Books.

Hume, David. 1985 [1777]. "Of the Standard of Taste." In *Essays Moral, Political, and Literary*. Indianapolis: Liberty Classics.

Humphries, Patrick. 1989. *Paul Simon: Still Crazy after All These Years*. New York: Doubleday.

Huntington, Samuel P. 1996. *The Clash of Civilizations and the Remaking of World Order*. New York: Simon and Schuster.

Ilott, Terry. 1996. *Budgets and Markets: A Study of the Budgeting of European Film*. New York: Routledge.

Irwin, Douglas A. 1996. *Against the Tide: An Intellectual History of Free Trade*. Princeton: Princeton University Press.

161

Issawi, Charles. 1980. *The Economic History of Turkey, 1800–1914*. Chicago: University of Chicago Press.

Iyer, Pico. 1989. *Video Night in Kathmandu*. New York: Vintage Books.

Jacobsen, Charles W. 1971. *Oriental Rugs: A Complete Guide*. Tokyo: Charles E. Tuttle.

James, Alison. 2001. "French Box Office Hits 20-Year Record." *Variety*, 5–11 March, 26.

James, George Wharton. 1974. *Indian Blankets and Their Makers*. Glorieta, N.M.: Rio Grande Press.

Jameson, Fredric. 2000. "Globalization and Strategy." *New Left Review*, July/August, 49–68.

Kaes, Anton. 1997. "The New German Cinema." In *The Oxford History of World Cinema*, edited by Geoffrey Nowell-Smith, 614–27. Oxford: Oxford University Press.

Kahlenberg, Mary Hunt. 1998. *The Extraordinary in the Ordinary*. New York: Harry N. Abrams.

Kahlenberg, Mary Hunt, and Anthony Berlant. 1972. *The Navajo Blanket*. Los Angeles: Praeger Publishers and Los Angeles County Museum of Art.

Kapp, Kit S. 1972. *Mola Art from the San Blas Islands*. K. S. Kapp Publications.

Kaufman, Alice, and Christopher Selser. 1985. *The Navajo Weaving Tradition: 1650 to the Present*. New York: E. P. Dutton.

Kazadi, Pierre. 1971. "Congo Music: Africa's Favorite Beat." *Africa Report*, April, 24–27.

———. 1973. "Trends of Nineteenth and Twentieth Century Music in the Congo-Zaire." In *Musikkulturen Asiens, Afrikas und Ozeaniens im 19. Jahrhundert*, edited by Robert Günther, 267–83. Regensburg, Germany: Gustav Bosse.

Kent, Kate Peck. 1976. "Pueblo and Navajo Weaving Traditions and the Western World." In *Ethnic and Tourist Arts: Cultural Expressions from the Fourth World*, edited by Nelson H. H. Graburn, 85–101. Berkeley: University of California.

———. 1985. *Navajo Weaving: Three Centuries of Change*. Santa Fe: School of American Research Press.

Khan, M. 1969. *An Introduction to the Egyptian Cinema*. London: Informatics.

Kim, Sukkoo. 1997. "Economic Integration and Convergence: U.S. Regions, 1840–1987." Working Paper 6335, National Bureau of Economic Research; Cambridge, Mass.

King, Donald. 1966. "Currents of Trade: Industries, Merchants and Money." In *The Flowering of the Middle Ages*, edited by Joan Evans, 199–230. New York: Bonanza Books.

King, J.C.H. 1986. "Tradition in Native American Art." In *The Arts of the North American Indian*, edited by Edwin L. Wade, 65–92. New York: Hudson Hill Press.

King, John. 1990. *Magical Reels: A History of Cinema in Latin America*. New York: Verso.

———. 1998. "Cinema." In *A Cultural History of Latin America. Literature, Music and the Visual Arts in the Nineteenth and Twentieth Centuries*, 455–518. Cambridge: Cambridge University Press.

Kinzer, Stephen. 1997. "From Splendid Isolation, Treasures for the World." *New York Times*, 16 September, A4.

Klein, Naomi. 2000. *No Space, No Jobs, No Logo: Taking Aim at the Brand Bullies*. New York: Picador USA.

Kolmel, Michael. 1985. " 'Economic Efficiency vs. Artistic Standard: The Case of Public Support for the Film Industry in West Germany." In *Governments and Culture*, edited by C. Richard Waits, William S. Hendon, and Harold Horowitz, 106–21. Akron: Association for Cultural Economists.

Komatsu, Hiroshi. 1997. "Japan: Before the Great Kanto Earthquake." In *The Oxford History of World Cinema*, edited by Geoffrey Nowell-Smith, 177–82. Oxford: Oxford University Press.

Krause, Richard Kraus. 1989. *Pianos and Politics in China: Middle-Class Ambitions and the Struggle over Western Music*. New York: Oxford University Press.

Kroeber, Alfred. 1969. *Configurations of Culture Growth*. Berkeley: University of California Press.

Krotz, Larry. 1996. *Tourists: How Our Fastest Growing Industry Is Changing the World*. Boston: Faber and Faber.

Krugman, Paul R. 1979. "Increasing Returns, Monopolistic Competition, and International Trade." *Journal of International Economics* 9:469–79.

———. 1980. "Scale Economies, Product Differentiation, and the Pattern of Trade." *American Economic Review* 70:950–59.

———. 1996. *Pop Internationalism*. Cambridge: MIT Press.

Kuisel, Richard. 1993. *Seducing the French: The Dilemma of Americanization*. Berkeley: University of California Press.

Kumar, Satish. 1996. "Gandhi's *Swadeshi*: The Economics of Permanence." In *The Case against the Global Economy, and for a Turn towards the Local*, edited by Jerry Mander and Edward Goldsmith, 418–24. San Francisco: Sierra Club Books.

Kymlicka, Will. 1995. *Multicultural Citizenship: A Liberal Theory of Minority Rights*. Oxford: Clarendon Press.

Lealand, Geoff. 1988. *A Foreign Egg in Our Nest? American Popular Culture in New Zealand*. Wellington: Victoria University Press.

Lencek, Lena, and Gideon Bosker. 1998. *The Beach: The History of Paradise on Earth*. New York: Viking.

Lent, John A. 1990. *The Asian Film Industry*. Austin: University of Texas Press.

Levenstein, Harvey. 1993. *Paradox of Plenty: A Social History of Eating in Modern America*. Oxford: Oxford University Press.

———. 1998. *Seductive Journey: American Tourists in France from Jefferson to the Jazz Age*. Chicago: University of Chicago Press.

Lévi-Strauss, Claude. 1976. *Structural Anthropology*. Vol. 2. New York: Basic Books.

Linder, Staffan Burenstam. 1970. *The Harried Leisure Class*. New York: Columbia University Press.

Lindig, Wolfgang. 1993. *Navajo: Tradition and Change in the Southwest*. New York: Facts on File.

Lipsitz, George. 1994. *Dangerous Crossroads: Popular Music, Postmodernism, and the Poetics of Place*. New York: Verso Books.

Lockhart, Laurence. 1958. *The Fall of the Safavi Dynasty and the Afghan Occupation of Persia*. Cambridge: At the University Press.

Lovejoy, Arthur O., and Arthur Boas. 1965. *Primitivism and Related Ideas in Antiquity*. New York: Octagon Books.

Lynton, Linda. 1995. *The Sari: Styles-Patterns-History-Techniques*. New York: Harry N. Abrams.

Macgowan, Kenneth. 1965. *Behind the Screen: The History and Techniques of the Motion Picture*. New York: Delacorte Press.

Magder, Ted. 1993. *Canada's Hollywood: The Canadian State and Feature Films*. Toronto: University of Toronto Press.

Maizels, John. 1996. *Raw Creation: Outsider Art and Beyond*. London: Phaidon Press.

Mannheim, Karl. 1952. "On the Interpretation of 'Weltanschauung.' " In *Essays on the Sociology of Knowledge*, 33–83. New York: Oxford University Press.

Manuel, Peter. 1988. *Popular Musics of the Non-Western World*. New York: Oxford University Press.

———. 1993. *Cassette Culture: Popular Music and Technology in North India*. Chicago: University of Chicago Press.

Mapp, Alf J., Jr. 1998. *Three Golden Ages: Discovering the Creative Secrets of Renaissance Florence, Elizabethan England, and America's Founding*. Lanham, Md.: Madison Books.

Marre, Jeremy, and Hannah Charlton. 1985. *Beats of the Heart: Popular Music of the World*. London: Pluto Press.

Mason, Peter. 1998. *Bacchanal! The Carnival Culture of Trinidad*. Philadelphia: Temple University Press.

Mathews, Kate. 1998. !*Molas*! Asheville, N.C.: Lark Books.

McDowell, Edwin. 1998. "Jumping on America's Hospitality Bandwagon." *New York Times*, 6 May, D1, D3.

McKean, Philip Frick. 1989. "Towards a Theoretical Analysis of Tourism: Economic Dualism and Cultural Involution in Bali." In *Hosts and*

*Guests: The Anthropology of Tourism*, edited by Valene L. Smith, 119–38. Philadelphia: University of Pennsylvania Press.

McNitt, Frank. 1962. *The Indian Traders*. Norman, Okla.: University of Oklahoma Press.

Maxwell, Robyn. 1990. *Textiles of Southeast Asia: Tradition, Trade, and Transformation*. Oxford: Oxford University Press.

Mehta, S. D. 1953. *The Indian Cotton Textile Industry: An Economic Analysis*. Bombay: The Textile Association.

Meintjes, Louise. 1990. "Paul Simon's Graceland, South Africa, and the Mediation of Musical Meaning." *Ethnomusicology* (Winter): 37–74.

Mensah, Atta Annan. 1980. "Music South of the Sahara." In *Musics of Many Cultures: An Introduction*, edited by Elizabeth May, 172–94. Berkeley: University of California Press.

Meurant, Georges. 1995. *Shoowa Design: African Textiles from the Kingdom of Kuba*. London: Thames and Hudson.

Micklethwait, John, and Adrian Wooldridge. 2000. *Future Perfect: The Challenge and Hidden Promise of Globalization*. New York: Crown Publishers.

Milanesi, Enza. 1993. *The Bulfinch Guide to Carpets*. Boston: Little, Brown, and Company.

Montesquieu, Charles Louis de Secondat baron de La Brede. 1965 [1748]. *Considerations on the Causes of the Greatness of the Romans and Their Decline*. Ithaca: Cornell University Press.

———. 1989 [1748]. *The Spirit of the Laws*. Cambridge: Cambridge University Press.

Morris, Morris D. 1969. "Trends and Tendencies in Indian Economic History." In *Indian Economy in the Nineteenth Century: A Symposium*, by Morris D. Morris, Toru Matsui, Bipin Chandra, and T. Raychaudhuri, 101–70. Delhi: Indian Economic and Social History Association.

———. 1983. "The Growth of Large-Scale Industry to 1947." In *The Cambridge Economic History of India*. Vol. 2, edited by Dharma Kumar, with the editorial assistance of Meghnad Desai, 553–676. Cambridge: Cambridge University Press.

Mukarovsky, Jan. 1970. *Aesthetic Function, Norm and Value as Social Facts*. Ann Arbor: University of Michigan Press, Michigan Slavic Contributions.

Mukuna, Kazadi wa. 1979-80. "The Origin of Zairean Modern Music: A Socio-Economic Aspect." *African Urban Studies* 6 (Winter): 31–39.

———. 1980. "Congolese Music." In *The New Grove Dictionary of Music and Musicians*, Vol. 4, edited by Stanley Sadie, 659–61. New York: Macmillan Publishers.

Munro, Thomas. n.d. *Evolution in the Arts and Other Theories of Culture History*. Cleveland: Cleveland Museum of Art.

Muscio, Giuliana. 2000. "Invasion and Counterattack: Italian and American Film Relations in the Postwar Period." In *"Here, There, and Everywhere": The Foreign Politics of American Popular Culture*, edited by Reinhold Wagnleitner and Elaine Tyler May, 116–31. Hanover and London: University Press of New England.

Navarro, Mireya. 2000. "Complaints to Spanish TV: Where Are the Americans?" *New York Times*, 21 August, A23.

Negrine, R., and S. Papathanassopoulos. 1990. *The Internationalisation of Television*. London: Pinter Publishers.

*New Oceania: Rediscovering Our Sea of Islands*. 1993. A. Suva, Fiji: University of the South Pacific.

Newcomb, Horace. 1996. "Other People's Fictions: Cultural Appropriation, Cultural Integrity, and International Media Strategies." In *Mass Media and Free Trade: NAFTA and Cultural Industries*, edited by Emile G. McAnany and Kenton T. Wilkinson, 92–109. Austin: University of Texas Press.

Noam, Eli. 1991. *Television in Europe*. New York: Oxford University Press.

Nunley, John. 1996. "The Beat Goes on: Recycling and Improvisation in the Steel Bands of Trinidad and Tobago." In *Recycled, Re-Seen: Folk Art from the Global Scrap Heap*, edited by Charlene Cerny and Suzanne Seriff, 130–39. New York: Harry N. Abrams.

Nussbaum, Martha. 1997. *Cultivating Humanity: A Classical Defense of Reform in Liberal Education*. Cambridge: Harvard University Press.

Orvell, Miles. 1995. *After the Machine: Visual Arts and the Erasing of Cultural Boundaries*. Jackson: University of Mississippi Press.

Owen, Roger. 1981. *The Middle East in the World Economy, 1800–1914*. London and New York: Methuen.

Pangle, Thomas. 1992. *The Ennobling of Democracy: The Challenge of the Postmodern Era*. Baltimore: Johns Hopkins Press.

Pareles, Jon. 1998. "A Pop Post-Modernist Gives Up on Irony." *New York Times*, Washington edition, 8 November. Arts and Leisure section, pt. 2, pp. 33, 40.

Parsons, Edward Alexander. 1952. *The Alexandrian Library: Glory of the Hellenic World*. Amsterdam: Elsevier Press.

Paterculus, Velleius. 1967 [A.D. 30]). *Compendium of Roman History*. Cambridge: Harvard University Press.

Pearson, Roberta. 1997. "Transitional Cinema." In *The Oxford History of World Cinema*, edited by Geoffrey Nowell-Smith, 23–42. Oxford: Oxford University Press.

Pells, Richard. 1997. *Not like Us: How Europeans Have Loved, Hated, and Transformed American Culture since World War II*. New York: Basic Books.

Phillips, Barty. 1994. *Tapestry*. London: Phaidon Press.

Pillsbury, Richard. 1998. *No Foreign Food: The American Diet in Time and Place.* Boulder, Colo.: Westview Press.

Porter, Michael E. 1990. *The Competitive Advantage of Nations.* New York: Free Press.

Puls, Herta. 1988. *Textiles of the Kuna Indians of Panama.* Aylesbury, England: Shire Publications.

Puttnam, David, with Neil Watson. 1998. *Movies and Money.* New York: Alfred A. Knopf.

Riceour, Paul. 1965. "Universal Civilization and National Cultures." In *History and Truth.* Evanston, Ill.: Northwestern University Press.

Richards, Greg. 1996a. "Introduction: Culture and Tourism in Europe." In *Cultural Tourism in Europe,* edited by Greg Richards, 3–18. Wallingford, England: CAB International.

———. 1996b. "Social Context of Cultural Tourism." In *Cultural Tourism in Europe,* edited by Greg Richards, 47–70. Wallingford, England: CAB International.

Richter, Anne. 1994. *The Arts and Crafts of Indonesia.* San Francisco: Chronicle Books.

Rifkin, Jeremy. 2000. *The Age of Access: The New Culture of Hypercapi talism, Where All of Life is a Paid-for Experience.* New York: Jeremy P. Tarcher/Putnam.

Roberts, John Storm. 1972. *Black Music of Two Worlds.* New York: William Morrow and Company.

Robertson, Roland. 1992. *Globalization: Social Theory and Global Culture.* London: Sage Publications.

Robinson, Deanna Campbell; Elizabeth B. Buck; and Marlene Cuthbert. 1991. *Music at the Margins: Popular Music and Global Cultural Diversity.* Newbury Park, Calif.: Sage Publications.

Rocker, Rudolf. 1978 [1937]. *Nationalism and Culture.* St. Paul: Michael E. Coughlin.

Rodee, Marian E. 1981. *Old Navajo Rugs: Their Development from 1900 to 1940.* Albuquerque: University of New Mexico Press.

Rodman, Selden. 1948. *Renaissance in Haiti: Popular Painters in the Black Republic.* New York: Pellegrini and Cudahy.

———. 1961. *Haiti: The Black Republic.* New York: Devin-Adair.

———. 1982. *Artists in Tune with Their World: Masters of Popular Art in the Americas and Their Relation to the Folk Tradition.* New York: Simon and Schuster.

———. 1988. *Where Art Is Joy: Haitian Art: The First Forty Years.* New York: Ruggles de Latour.

Romanowski, William D. 1996. *Pop Culture Wars: Religion and the Role of Entertainment in American Life.* Downers Grove, Ill.: InterVarsity Press.

Rosenberg, Emily S. 1982. *Spreading the American Dream: American Economic and Cultural Expansion, 1890–1945*. New York: Hill and Wang.

Roud, Richard. 1993. *A Passion for Films: Henri Langlois and the Cinémathèque Française*. New York: Viking Press.

Sadowski, Yahya. 1998. *The Myth of Global Chaos*. Washington, D.C.: Brookings Institution Press.

Salvador, Mari Lyn. 1976. "The Clothing Arts of the Cuna of San Blas, Panama." In *Ethnic and Tourist Arts: Cultural Expressions from the Fourth World*, edited by Nelson H. H. Graburn, 165–82. Berkeley: University of California Press.

Santoro, Gene. 1993. "Borrowed Beats: Cuban Dance Rhythms Have Ignited American Music since the Turn of the Century." *Atlantic Monthly*, September, 96–100.

Savile, Anthony. 1982. *The Test of Time: An Essay in Philosophical Aesthetics*. Oxford: Clarendon Press.

Schiller, Herbert I. 1992. *Mass Communications and American Empire*. Boulder, Colo.: Westview Press.

Schivelbusch, Wolfgang. 1977. *The Railway Journey: Trains and Travel in the Nineteenth Century*. New York: Urizen Books.

Schlereth, Thomas J. 1977. *The Cosmopolitan Ideal in Enlightenment Thought*. Notre Dame, Ind.: University of Notre Dame Press.

Schnitman, Jorge A. 1984. *Film Industries in Latin America: Dependency and Development*. Norwood, N.J.: Ablex Publishing.

Segrave, Kerry. 1997. *American Films Abroad: Hollywood's Domination of the World's Movie Screens*. Jefferson, N.C.: McFarland and Company.

Shenk, David. 1997. *Data Smog: Surviving the Information Glut*. San Francisco: HarperEdge.

Shils, Edward. 1981. *Tradition*. Chicago: University of Chicago Press.

Sinclair, R. K. 1988. *Democracy and Participation in Athens*. Cambridge: Cambridge University Press.

Singhal, D. P. 1969. *India and World Civilization*. Vols. 1 and 2. Lansing, Mich.: Michigan State University Press.

Sinha, Sasadhar. 1962. *Social Thinking of Rabindranath Tagore*. London: Asia Publishing Guide.

Sklar, Robert. 1975. *Movie-Made America: A Social History of American Movies*. New York: Random House.

Sokolov, Raymond. 1991. *Why We Eat What We Eat*. New York: Simon and Schuster.

Spencer, Herbert. 1972. "Advice to the Modernizers of Japan." *Herbert Spencer on Social Evolution*, edited and with an introduction by J.D.Y. Peel, 253–57. Chicago: University of Chicago Press.

Stapledon, Chris, and Chris May. 1987. *African Rock: The Pop Music of a Continent*. New York: Dutton.

Stead, William T. 1901. *The Americanization of the World or the Trend of the Twentieth Century.* New York: Horace Markley.

Stewart, Gary. 2000. *Rumba on the River: A History of the Popular Music of the Two Congos.* New York: Verso.

Stewart, Hilary. 1990. *Totem Poles.* Seattle: University of Washington Press.

Stipp, H. 1993. "New Ways to Reach Children." *American Demographics* (August): 48–49.

Stone-Miller, Rebecca. 1992. *To Weave for the Arts: Andean Textiles in the Museum of Fine Arts, Boston.* Boston: Museum of Fine Arts.

Stuempfle, Stephen. 1995. *The Steelband Movement: The Forging of a National Art in Trinidad and Tobago.* Philadelphia: University of Pennsylvania Press.

Sturtevant, William C. 1986. "The Meanings of Native American Art." In *The Arts of the North American Indian,* edited by Edwin L. Wade, 23–44. New York: Hudson Hill Press.

Sutton, R. Anderson. 1985. "Commercial Cassette Recordings of Traditional Music in Java: Implications for Performers and Scholars." *The World of Music* 27:23–45.

Swain, Margaret Byrne. 1989. "Gender Roles in Indigenous Tourism: Kuna Mola, Kuna Yala, and Cultural Survival." In *Hosts and Guests: The Anthropology of Tourism,* edited by Valene L. Smith, 83–104. Philadelphia: University of Pennsylvania Press.

Swallow, D. A. 1982. "Production and Control in the Indian Garment Export Industry." In *From Craft to Industry: The Ethnography of Proto-Industrial Cloth Production,* edited by Esther N. Goody, 133–65. Cambridge: Cambridge University Press.

Swallow, Deborah. 1990. "The Raj: India 1850–1900." In *Arts of India: 1550–1900,* edited by Rosemary Crill, John Guy, Veronica Murphy, Susan Stronge, and Deborah Swallow, 209–28. London: Victoria and Albert Museum.

Sweeney, Philip. 1991. *The Virgin Directory of World Music.* New York: Henry Holt and Company.

Swinton, George. 1972. *Sculpture of the Eskimo.* Greenwich, Conn.: New York Graphic Society.

Taine, Hippolyte Adolphe. 1980 [1865]. *Philosophy of Art.* Ann Arbor: University Microfilms.

Tarlo, Emma. 1996. *Clothing Matters: Dress and Identity in India.* Chicago: University of Chicago Press.

Taylor, Timothy D. 1997. *Global Pop: World Music, World Markets.* New York: Routledge.

Teo, Stephen. 1997. *Hong Kong Cinema: The Extra Dimensions.* London: British Film Institute.

Thompson, Jon. 1988. *Oriental Carpets: From the Tents, Cottages and Workshops of Asia.* New York: E. P. Dutton.

Thompson, Kristin. 1985. *Exporting Entertainment: America in the World Film Market 1907–34*. London: BFI Publishing.

Tocqueville, Alexis de. 1969 [1835]. *Democracy in America*. New York: Harper and Row.

Tomlinson, John. 1991. *Cultural Imperialism: A Critical Introduction*. Baltimore: Johns Hopkins University Press.

———. 1999. *Globalization and Culture*. Chicago: University of Chicago Press.

Towse, Ruth, ed. 1997. *Baumol's Cost Disease: The Arts and Other Victims*. Cheltenham, England: Edward Elgar Press.

Tunstall, Jeremy. 1977. *Media Are American*. New York: Columbia University Press.

Turner, Louis, and John Ash. 1975. *The Golden Hordes*. London: Constable.

Twitchell, James B. 1992. *Carnival Culture: The Trashing of Taste in America*. Columbia University Press.

Underhill, Ruth M. 1956. *The Navajos*. Norman, Okla.: University of Oklahoma Press.

Urry, John. 1990. *The Tourist Gaze: Leisure and Travel in Contemporary Societies*. London: Sage Publications.

Usabel, Gaizka S. 1982. *The High Noon of American Films in Latin America*. Ann Arbor: UMI Research Press.

Usai, Paolo Cherchi. 1997. "Origins and Survival." In *The Oxford History of World Cinema*, edited by Geoffrey Nowell-Smith, 6–13. Oxford: Oxford University Press.

Vasey, Ruth. 1997a. *The World According to Hollywood, 1918–1939*. Madison: University of Wisconsin Press.

———. 1997b. "The World-Wide Spread of Cinema." In *The Oxford History of World Cinema*, edited by Geoffrey Nowell-Smith, 53–62. Oxford: Oxford University Press.

Victoria and Albert Museum. 1982. *The Indian Heritage: Court Life and Arts under Mughal Rule*. London: Victoria and Albert Museum.

Wagar, W. Warren. 1963. *The City of Man: Prophecies of a World Civilization in Twentieth-Century Thought*. Boston: Houghton Mifflin Company.

Waldron, Jeremy. 1996. "Multiculturalism and Mélange." In *Public Education in a Multicultural Society: Policy, Theory, Critique*, edited by Robert K. Fullinwider, 90–118. Cambridge: Cambridge University Press.

Walker, Daniel. 1997. *Flowers Underfoot: Indian Carpets of the Mughal Era*. New York: Metropolitan Museum of Art.

Wallis, Roger, and Krister Malm. 1984. *Big Sounds from Small Peoples: The Music Industry in Small Countries*. London: Constable.

Wangermée, Robert. 1991. *Cultural Policy in France*. Strasbourg: Council of Europe.

Warmington, E. H. 1974. *Commerce between the Roman Empire and India*. London: Curzon Press.

Warneke, Sara. 1995. *Images of the Educational Traveller in Early Modern England*. Leiden: E. J. Brill.

Warner, Keith Q. 1985. *Kaiso! The Trinidad Calypso: A Study of the Calypso as Oral Literature*. Washington, D.C.: Three Continents Press.

Waterbury, Ronald. 1989. "Embroidery for Tourists: A Contemporary Putting-Out System in Oaxaca, Mexico." In *Cloth and Human Experience*, edited by Annette B. Weiner and Jane Schneider, Washington, D.C.: Smithsonian Institution Press. 243–71.

Waterman, Christopher A. 1985. "Juju." In *The Western Impact on World Music: Change, Adaptation, and Survival*, edited by Bruno Nettl, 87–90. New York: Schirmer Books.

———. 1991. "Jùjú History: Toward a Theory of Sociomusical Practice." In *Ethnomusicology and Modern Music History*, edited by Stephen Blum, Philip V. Bohlman, and Daniel M. Neumann, 49–67. Urbana, Ill.: University of Illinois Press.

Waters, Malcolm. 1995. *Globalization*. London: Routledge.

Weatherford, Jack. 1988. *Indian Givers: How the Indians of the Americas Transformed the World*. New York: Crown Publishers.

———. 1994. *Savages and Civilization: Who Will Survive?* New York: Crown Publishers.

Weitzman, Martin L. 1992. "On Diversity." *Quarterly Journal of Economics*, 107, no. 2 (May): 363–405.

———. 1993. "What to Preserve? An Application of Diversity Theory to Crane Conservation." *Quarterly Journal of Economics* 108, no. 1 (February): 157–83.

Wells, G. A. 1959. *Herder and After: A Study in the Development of Sociology*. 'S-Gravenhage, Netherlands: Mouton and Co.

Wild, Lee S. 1987. "Hawaiian Quilts." In *America's Glorious Quilts*, edited by Dennis Duke and Deborah Harding, 134–51. Hong Kong: Hugh Lauter Levin.

Williams, Alan. 1992. *Republic of Images: A History of French Filmmaking*. Cambridge: Harvard University Press.

Withey, Lynne. 1987. *Voyages of Discovery: Captain Cook and the Exploration of the Pacific*. New York: William Morrow and Company.

———. 1997. *Grand Tours and Cook's Tours: A History of Leisure Travel, 1750 to 1915*. New York: William Morrow and Company.

Woodcock, George. 1977. *Peoples of the Coast: The Indians of the Pacific Northwest*. Bloomington: Indiana University Press.

Wright, Richard E., and John T. Wertime. 1995. *Caucasian Carpets and Covers*. London: Hali Publications.

Wright, Ronald. 1992. *Stolen Continents: The "New World" through Indian Eyes*. Boston: Houghton Mifflin.

# ◼◼ Index